Lonely planet Kids

Wild Things

Jo Schofield & Fiona Danks

Illustrations by Pete Williamson

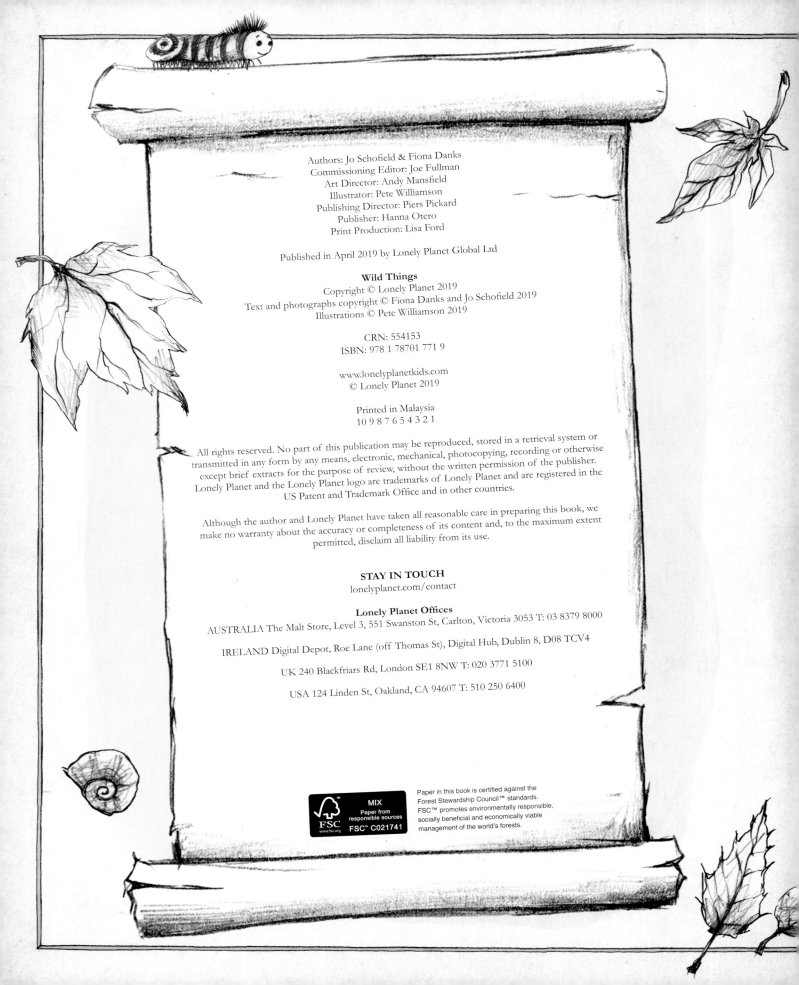

Authors: Jo Schofield & Fiona Danks
Commissioning Editor: Joe Fullman
Art Director: Andy Mansfield
Illustrator: Pete Williamson
Publishing Director: Piers Pickard
Publisher: Hanna Otero
Print Production: Lisa Ford

Published in April 2019 by Lonely Planet Global Ltd

Wild Things

CRN: 554153
ISBN: 978 1 78701 771 9

www.lonelyplanetkids.com
© Lonely Planet 2019

Printed in Malaysia
10 9 8 7 6 5 4 3 2 1

STAY IN TOUCH
lonelyplanet.com/contact

Lonely Planet Offices
AUSTRALIA The Malt Store, Level 3, 551 Swanston St, Carlton, Victoria 3053 T: 03 8379 8000

IRELAND Digital Depot, Roe Lane (off Thomas St), Digital Hub, Dublin 8, D08 TCV4

UK 240 Blackfriars Rd, London SE1 8NW T: 020 3771 5100

USA 124 Linden St, Oakland, CA 94607 T: 510 250 6400

Meet the authors

Jo Schofield and Fiona Danks have written a selection of books packed full of activities to inspire children and families to get outdoors, have fun and discover the wonders of the natural world. Through these titles and their website (www. goingwild.net) they aim to raise awareness of the many benefits children gain by interacting and reconnecting with wild places – whether up a mountain or in the local park. They also work in partnership with UK environmental and educational organisations and charities, making outdoor play and environmental education more accessible to a wider audience. They both live in Oxfordshire with their families.

Contents

Discovering
Wild Things

Have you ever wanted to spy on fairies in the garden, meet a unicorn, ride a dragon or share a picnic with a mermaid? Just because you've never seen these creatures doesn't mean they don't exist. The Wild Things of stories and the imagination are everywhere, but they are shy, secretive and camouflaged – and only reveal themselves to true believers.

This fantastical guidebook will help you find them by unlocking the magical power of nature. Look for Wild Things in forests, meadows and fields, in ponds, rivers and at the seaside. You can also find them in everyday places: in school playgrounds, local parks, or among the pots on the patio. Shape-shift through real and imaginary worlds where every hollow tree leads to another planet, every stream is made of silver and magical forces whisper through the forest.

You can discover the mysteries of nature all year round and at any time of day or night. So switch your imagination onto full blast, learn to use all your senses, brush up on your magic skills and take a giant leap into the world of the Wild Things.

Wild Things survival Kit

Here's some of the cool equipment you can take with you on your Wild Things adventures. You should also pack a first-aid kit, just in case you are unlucky enough to fall off your dragon or be bitten by an angry fairy.

Plaster of Paris for footprint casts

String, scissors and double-sided tape

Clay for making magical creatures

Mirror for secret messages and seeing what's behind you

Head torch (add red cellophane for spying on night creatures)

A blindfold for practising sensory skills

Magnifying glass and bug box to help you shrink and see into miniature worlds

Magical equipment: a broomstick for speedy travel, a magic wand, a spell book and a spy stone to peep into other worlds

Charcoal and chalk for trails and secret messages

Bags and bottles for collecting natural treasures; bottles for potions and spells

Binoculars to see the faraway Wild Things

Cat food for Wild Things bait

Hats for shade or warmth

Sun cream (best to use unperfumed so monsters don't smell you coming)

Drinking water and tasty snacks – you never know when you will get your next meal!

Wild skills training

You and your friends may be able to zap aliens in virtual worlds but how long would you last outside in the real wild world? Wild skills training will get you ready to immerse yourself in nature's magic.

Did you know that nature's Wild Things have superpowers? Grasshoppers jump so high it's as if we could jump over a house, bees smell nectar up to 2 km (1.25 miles) away and ants carry such heavy weights it's like a human carrying a car.

Human powers may seem pretty feeble in comparison but, by following these lessons to develop your wild senses and skills, you will find your way in the wild world of nature and the imagination – where anything is possible.

So switch off the virtual world, get outside and become a brave wild explorer.

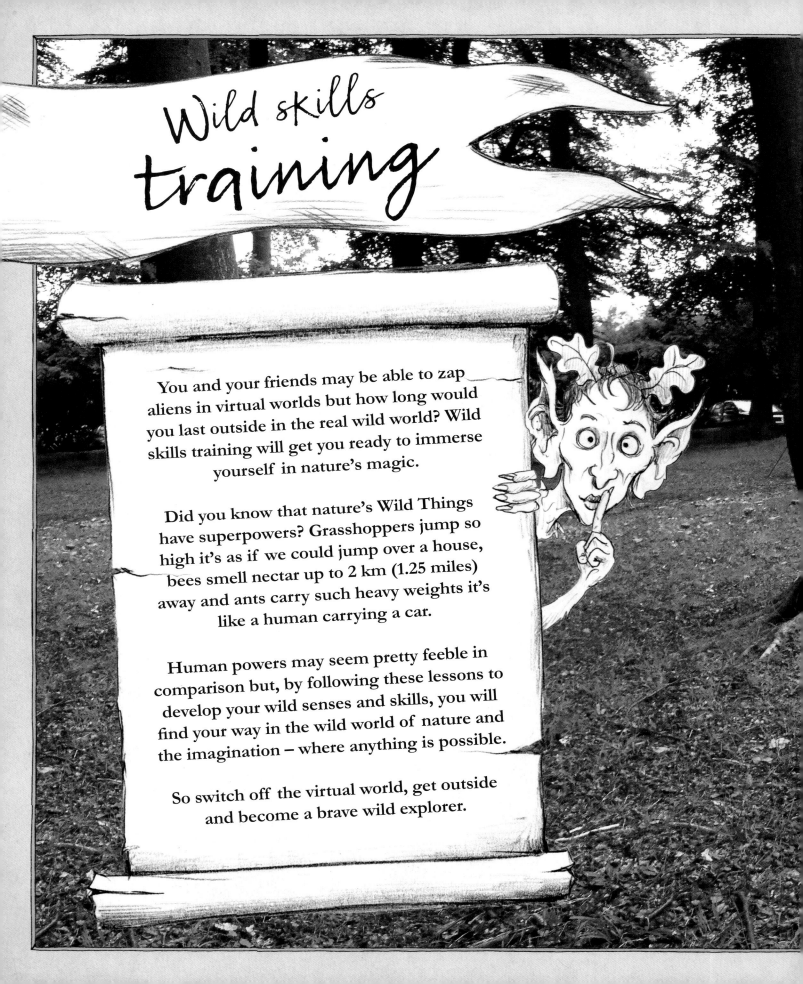

Lesson 1: Staying safe

Run free, have adventures, test your limits and enjoy challenges, but, above all, stay safe! Wherever you are in the wild world, you need to make sure you look after yourself, your companions and your environment.

Grown-up guidance

Never attempt anything that may be dangerous without grown-up help. This means having an adult present during any activity that involves exploring (especially near water), cutting, tasting (particularly anything gathered from the wild), burning or the use of hot materials.

Wild safety

Different places have different dangers, so make sure you know all the ones that may arise where your adventure is taking place – as well as the necessary safety precautions.

Be aware of any poisonous plants or dangerous animals where you are exploring. Never collect poisonous plants, fungi or berries.

Tell someone at once if you are bitten or stung.

Always take extra care when playing in – or exploring near – water.

Check for ticks after playing outdoors. Always seek medical treatment if bitten by a tick.

Keep cuts covered and always wash hands after playing in wild water and working with natural materials.

If going foraging for edible fruits, leaves and nuts, make sure you know exactly what is safe to eat.

Only use knives with grown-up supervision.

Always have a first-aid kit handy, and make sure you're with someone who knows how to use it.

Fire safety

Fire can be magical and mesmerising, but always follow this guidance:

Never make fire unless you have permission to do so, and there are grown-ups around to supervise.

Make fires well away from overhanging trees and buildings.

Make fire on mineral soil, in a pit or preferably in a metal fire pan.

Never light a fire in windy or very dry weather.

Never leave a fire unattended.

Have a supply of water nearby to extinguish the fire or soothe burns.

Use as little wood as you can and let the fire burn down to ash.

Once the ashes are completely cold, remove all traces of your fire.

Looking after the wild world

Leave no trace. True Wild Thing explorers always leave wild places as they found them. Never leave anything behind in the wild world that doesn't belong there. Take all litter home with you.

Learn your local foraging laws. Some plants may be protected and so shouldn't be picked. If in doubt, leave it alone.

Only collect loose wild materials that are common and plentiful.

Do not trespass on private property or take anything without the landowner's permission.

When foraging for wild foods, don't be greedy. Leave plenty for the Wild Things.

Be considerate of other people enjoying wild places.

Wild Things live everywhere – look after them and protect their homes.

Lesson 2: Wild senses

The first thing you need to do, if you're to make the most of the natural world, is to sharpen up your wild senses.

Wild sight

Our eyes may look, but how much do they really see? Discover how to peer into the heart of the wild world. You may even spot things that aren't quite what they seem…

Looking up close

Use a magnifying glass to check out nature's tiny wonders.

Is that leaf an elf's map?

Is that red thorn a bloody dagger from an elf battle?

Are those tiny flecks of ice or glittering fairy diamonds?

Is that little stone a troll's decaying tooth?

Looking far away

Allow your eyes to gaze far away into the distance. If you look through half-closed eyes, you may spot some surprises!

Is that faraway island mountain a sleeping giant?

Is that fluffy white cloud a monster's head?

Is that early morning fog or a dragon's smoky breath?

Looking in the dark

When we are tucked up in our beds at night, the wild world comes alive. To see Wild Things at night, try not to use a torch at first. After a few minutes, your eyes will adjust and your natural night sight will show you shapes, shadows and surprising details.

Red light night sight

Night sight is best, but if you have to use a torch, try to make it a red one, as most Wild Things can't see red light. Use a head torch to keep your hands free.

Cellophane wrapped sweet

Cellophane rainbow!

1. Attach red cellophane to a head torch with an elastic band.

2. Go on a night expedition – your red light won't scare wild creatures away.

3. Experiment with different colours. What does the world look like through each one?

4. For a fun night-time game, give everyone a different coloured head torch and play dark tag.

Training your eyes to look for wild materials

Loose wild materials are found everywhere, from the wild woods to city streets. You may find fallen leaves, petals, twigs and seeds, empty shells, lost feathers and who knows what else.

Always look carefully at loose materials. Try to imagine what they may become:

This fireweed monster has a red leaf tongue and sticky burr eyes.

This woodland dragon has fiery breath (a red leaf), a beady eye (an acorn), scaly legs (pine cones) and a wooden head.

You never know what wild treasures you may find, so always have a collecting bag or box at the ready.

Safety tips
• All loose wild materials are precious. Only collect small quantities of commonly found materials that are safe to gather.
• When no longer required, return unused materials to a place where they can rot down.

Taste, smell and touch

To fully enjoy the Wild Things' world, don't just rely on your eyes – get tasting, smelling and touching too!

Wild tasting game

Test you and your friends' wild sense of taste.

1. Collect some wild foods, prepare them and arrange them on a plate. Mashing them up will confuse the tasters!

2. Each taster should wear a blindfold and hold their nose so they can concentrate on the taste buds! Can they identify the tastes?

3. For extra fun, prepare funny labels, like the ones on this plate.

4. Include one type of shop-bought food. Can anyone guess which is the odd one out?

Wild taste

Discover delicious wild tastes on a foraging adventure, but take along a grown-up who knows exactly which leaves, berries and nuts are safe to eat. Wild foods, particularly berries, make wonderful edible potions (see page 42).

You will need:
Wild foods, a plate, a spoon and a blindfold.

Sea serpent eggs (elderberries)

Secret ingredient for a witch's spell (wild marjoram)

Squidgy eyeballs (wild plums)

Fairy chewing gum (chopped mint leaves)

Congealed dragon blood (mashed-up blackberries)

Troll spit (stewed wild apple)

Safety tips
• Always have a grown-up with you when collecting wild tastes.
• Wash wild foods before eating.
• Never eat anything if you aren't absolutely certain it is safe to eat.
• Only forage in wild places away from roads and other sources of pollution.

Wild smell

Dogs can't read newspapers, so they sniff the air to find out what's been going on in the world. All Wild Things rely on smell to find their way around, recognise friends, identify enemies and mark territories.

Smelling test

Wild places are full of good and bad smells. Have you ever smelt the rain coming, the sweet scent of freshly cut grass, or the salty tang of the seaside? If you shut your eyes, do the smells become stronger? Try this smelling test to improve your natural sniffing ability.

The warmer your jars are, the more odours they will release.

You will need:

Jam jars with lids, a tray and a cloth, blindfolds and smelly wild materials.

1. Collect wild materials with a range of smells. This test includes wet soil, rosemary, mint, freshly cut grass and dried grass. Throw everyone off the scent by giving your materials Wild Thing names. Imagine smelling fairy tea leaves or goblin toothpaste!

2. Put one material in each jar and close the lid. Place the jars on a tray somewhere warm, preferably outdoors in the sunshine. The warmth will bring out the smell.

3. Hide the jars under a cloth.

4. Put your friends to the test. Give them a blindfold and ask them to put it over their eyes before smelling each jar. Can they identify each smell?

Wild touch

Feel the wild world with your hands, your feet, your face or even your whole body! Experience the touch of wind, rain and sunshine, and lie on the ground to feel the earth beneath you.

Fearsome feely boxes

Are you brave enough to put your hand into a monster's mouth and let your fingers discover mystery objects?

1. Gather together some wild materials. This feely box contains a witch's finger (a knobbly stick), a monster's toenail (a shell), and a dragon's egg (a plane tree seed).

2. Make the cardboard box into a monster's head with a gaping mouth big enough for you to reach inside. Stick it together with hot glue and add big eyes, twiggy teeth and grassy hair.

3. Cut a little doorway in the back of the box so you can sneak the mystery objects inside.

4. Can your friends work out what they are feeling?

5. To up the fun, add some scary things, like these dragon's eyes – walnut shell eye sockets with tomato eyeballs.

Feel the world with your feet

For a real sensory adventure, go barefoot. Wade through a muddy puddle, walk over a soft mossy tussock or crunch over a leafy woodland floor. If you're feeling brave, you could ask a trusted friend to lead you on a barefoot blindfold walk in the wild. Let the soles of your feet tell you about the world.

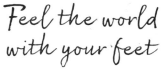

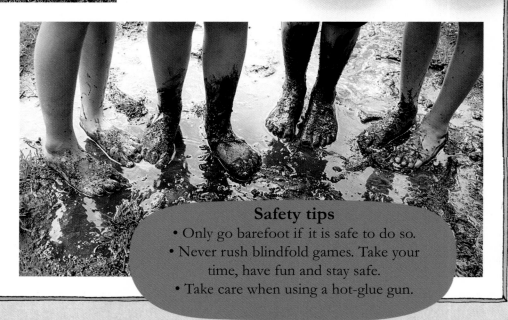

Safety tips
- Only go barefoot if it is safe to do so.
- Never rush blindfold games. Take your time, have fun and stay safe.
- Take care when using a hot-glue gun.

Wild sounds

Our lives are full of noise: voices, cars, television, music and all sorts of electronic sounds. Wild Thing explorers tune in to a different kind of listening. Wherever you are, let the wild sounds in. Even in the city you may be surprised by what you can hear.

Wild recording

- Use a mobile device to play or record the sounds and calls of the wild.
- Play a bird song on a mobile device. Will a real bird or a Wild Thing respond?
- Record wild sounds – perhaps the dawn chorus or the sound of breaking waves could become your morning alarm or soothe you to sleep at night.

Tuning in to wild sounds

In spring or summer, find a wild place, lie down and shut your eyes. What can you hear?
- Wind whispering secrets • Insects buzzing
- Birds singing • Rain pitter-pattering • Waves breaking • Seeds popping • Fairies fluttering
- Trolls trumping • Giants snoring • Monsters' feet snapping twigs in the undergrowth.

Listening games

Try these games to get your ears tuned in to listening.

You will need:
Blindfolds, a water pistol, and crunchy empty packets.

Bat and moth

Discover how bats use echolocation to track down their prey. One person is a bat and another is the moth, while everyone else stands in a circle around them. The bat is blindfolded and has to find the moth by calling out "bat" to which the moth has to reply "moth". Can the bat catch the moth? Everyone else helps the bat to stay within the circle.

Sneaking game

This is a great way to learn how to sneak up on a Wild Thing without it hearing you! Everyone sits in a circle around a noisy object, such as an empty crisp packet. One person (the listener) is blindfolded and stands in the middle armed with a water pistol. Another person (the sneak) creeps into the middle of the circle, picks up the packet and creeps back. But watch out, if the listener hears anything, he or she will fire water at the sneak. To make it more of a challenge, make the sneak wear a bell!

Scavenger stories

Collect wild treasures on a walk. Can you use them to make up a story, like this twiggy tale?

Once upon a time, a lonely boy with a broken leg limped into the forest (1), leaning heavily on a walking stick (2). A giant bird (3) flew down, grabbed the stick in its talons (4) and knocked the boy over. The boy was upset but, as he lay in the forest, he began to notice the wild world around him. He saw a snake shedding its skin (5) and found a tiny catapult (6) among the leaves. Suddenly, an elf appeared, grabbed the catapult and with a flick of his magic wand (7) fixed the boy's leg. But instead of rushing home, the boy stayed for hours, discovering more of the forest's magical secrets.

1

2

3

4

5

6

7

Release your 6th sense. Wild imagination

Have you ever had a creepy feeling that you were being watched or that you have been in a place before? This weird feeling is perhaps a sixth sense, a way into the world of the imagination and a belief that anything is possible. Open the door to wonder and other worlds through storytelling and imaginary games.

Story box

Fill a special box with wild treasures and a few favourite things. Pass the box round a circle of friends. Each person takes something out and adds to the story.

Story stones

Decorate smooth pebbles with symbols and pictures of Wild Things. Put them in a special bag, then pick them out randomly and weave them into a story.

Spy stones

Have you ever wanted to peep into other worlds? Then what you need is a magical spy stone – but first, you have to find one.

You will need:
Stones with holes, marker pens, coloured pencils or paint.

1. Hunt for an ancient stone with a hole. The best places to find them are beaches, beside rivers or in flinty soils.

2. Your stone has acquired its magic over millions of years, moulded by the power of water and ice. Imagine the stories it could tell, what it has seen during its long lifetime, and what it might allow you to see.

3. Decorate your stone with permanent marker pens, coloured pencils and/or paints. Choose a design that's special to you. The more you work on it, the more magical it will become.

4. Take your stone on every wild adventure, but keep it safe! You never know what secrets it might show you.

You could turn your stone into an all-seeing eye, like this one.

Or perhaps your stone could be a serpent or a one-eyed monster.

Spy holes

There are spy holes everywhere in the wild world. Look for them in pieces of ice, in trees and even in rocks. Peep through spy holes and you may discover wild secrets, or spot monsters, fairies or other Wild Things.

Doorways and portals into other worlds

Every wild place is crowded with secret doorways and magical portals. Add a touch of wild imagination and they will swing open, leading you to endless adventures, new worlds and parallel universes where anything might be possible.

Magic carpets

This is a hair-raising way to travel wherever your imagination wishes to go in the blink of an eye!

Magic carpets are almost impossible to find, so weave one of your own on the forest floor.

Find a space on the ground in a clearing, then open your imagination and make a wild design with locally gathered leaves, seeds and nuts.

This dragon carpet with long tassels and a control stick will outfly the fastest dragon!

How many entries to other worlds can you discover?
Look for pathways through trees, holes in hedges, tunnels
under bridges, seaside doorways or holes in the ground.

Make your own doorways and portals in
different places, like this woven portal
between two trees.

Lesson 3:
Spying

Blend in with the wild world to improve your chances of spotting Wild Things and imaginary creatures. But beware, they have eyes that see all around, noses that sniff every suspicious scent and ears that hear the slightest crackle among the leaves. Follow these tips to become a wild world spy.

Move quietly

Even the most enormous Wild Things move almost silently through wild spaces. Catch them unawares by keeping the noise down (see the Sneaking Game, page 21). Don't chatter, move slowly and tread lightly.

Wear spy clothes

Dress carefully in natural colours, non-rustly fabric and soft-soled shoes. Hide the shape of your face and head with smears of mud and a scarf or a hat. Put your outfit to the test – can your friends spot you lying among the plants when they walk past?

Put on wild camouflage

Use some wild camouflage to blend into the wild world.

You will need:

Garden netting, raffia, a bicycle helmet, elastic, cardboard and double-sided tape.

Camouflage crown or helmet

Cover a bike helmet with leaves tucked into elastic, or stick leaves onto a cardboard crown covered in double-sided tape.

Camouflage cape

Make a cape from garden netting. Weave locally gathered wild materials through the netting, or tie them on with brown string or raffia.

Mask your smell

Time to be natural! Ask your grown-ups to use unscented laundry liquid. Don't use scented shampoo. Rub yourself with mud or sweet-smelling herbs to mask your smell.

Lesson 4: Wild world navigation

Some birds and insects fly thousands of miles to reach their feeding and nesting places. Their natural navigational superpowers show them the way with the help of the sun, the stars, the moon, air currents, natural landmarks and even smells in the air. It's time to practise your own natural navigation and mapping skills.

Make a leaf compass

This is a quick and easy way to make a compass and find which way is north.

You will need:

A leaf, a stainless steel sewing needle, a magnet and a puddle of still water.

1. Magnetise the needle by stroking it several times in the same direction with the magnet.

2. Find a leaf big enough for the needle to lie on, and place it on a puddle out of the wind.

3. Put the needle on the leaf. Watch as the leaf turns in the water until the needle points north.

4. Not sure if it's working? Check it against a real compass or a compass app on a phone!

Three-dimensional treasure map

You will need:

Clay, coins for treasure, wild materials and a tray.

Try this mapping game in the woods. Hide the treasure with a little twig and clay elf in a small wild area (about the size of a room!). On the ground nearby or on a tray, create a miniature elf-scale 3D map of the area using soil, twigs, leaves and seeds to represent the earth, trees, logs and smaller plants. Place a coin on the 3D map to show where the treasure is hidden in the real world. Who can find the treasure?

Treasure-box trail

You will need:

Maps, treasure boxes, and a compass.

This is a real test of your map-reading skills! Ask an adult to make a trail, hiding treasure boxes to find on the way. Can you and your friends find the treasure boxes by reading the map, using a compass and following the Wild Things clues? You might follow the unicorn hoof prints up the hill, look for a fairy's red flag in a leafy canopy or find treasure being protected by a dragon.

Lesson 5:
Tracking

The best way to find Wild Things is to follow the clues they leave behind.

Reading tracks and signs

You'll see clues and tracks of Wild Things everywhere. But can you work out what they mean?

Footprints – is that paw print a dog or a dragon? Is that hoof print a pony or a unicorn?

Animal poo – is that smelly poo in a hole in the soil from a badger or a troll?

Fur – is that tuft of fur caught on a wire fence from a deer or a goblin?

Feathers – is that pile of feathers the dinner remains of a fox or a giant?

Practise tracking in wet mud or snow where it's easy to spot tracks. Once you know what to look for, try looking in other places. Throw other trackers off the scent by making a mystery track trail with a plaster of Paris dragon or monster print you made earlier (see page 130).

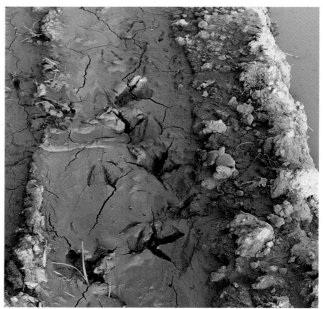

Who left these tracks in soft mud?
Was it a large bird?
Or a small dragon?

Make a magical tracking stick

Imagine following unicorn tracks through the woods until you find the magical creature. This tracking stick trains your eyes to look for the faintest tracks. The bigger the gap between each track, the faster the Wild Thing was running (or the longer its legs!).

You will need:

A magic stick, elastic bands, a pen knife, a tape measure, and a permanent marker pen.

1. Choose a strong, straight stick. One with a V-shaped handle can double up as a walking stick and staff.

2. Measure 4 cm (1.5 in) intervals along the stick, marking each one. Then carefully scrape the bark off the stick in alternate 4 cm (1.5 in) bands.

3. Add marks in each band with the knife or a permanent marker pen.

4. To add the magic, decorate with wild materials and draw a spooky face.

5. Roll two elastic bands on to the stick. Use these to mark the distance between two tracks. This will help you find where the next track should be. Now you're ready to go tracking!

Safety tip
• Only use a knife with a grown-up's help.

Stay safe – always cut away from you.

Hold the stick up to the track to measure it.

White stone trail

Follow a pebble trail like Hansel and Gretel to fine-tune your tracking skills. Get a friend to drop numbered white pebbles in some long grass, all about the same distance from each other. The longer the grass, the harder the tracking, but your tracking stick should help you find all the pebbles.

Numbering your stones will let your trackers realise if they've missed one. If it's too easy, try spacing the stones farther apart.

Arrow trails

This game will improve your tracking skills. One team (the trailblazers) lays a trail of arrows and hides, then a second team (the trackers) follows the trail to hunt them down. Every time the trailblazers change direction, they must make or draw an arrow to show where they've gone. Here are a few arrow-trail ideas:

You will need:

Sticks, stones, natural thorns, a black marker pen, flour, squeezy plastic bottles, food colouring and water.

Natural arrows
- Make arrows with sticks, stones, mud, chalk or ice.
- Draw arrows on rocks with a stone or charcoal.

Flour trails

Borrow some flour from the kitchen to leave a trail of floury arrows. They are biodegradable and edible so won't stay there for long.

Leaf trails

1. Draw arrows on several leaves using a marker pen.
2. Pin the leaves on to tree trunks with thorns or pointed sticks, making a trail to follow.

Arrows in the snow

1. On a snowy day, fill plastic bottles with water and add enough natural food colouring to make a strong colour.
2. Go outside and squirt the bottles at the snow to draw arrows or leave secret messages (see page 34).

Lesson 6:
Secret codes and messages

Perhaps you could leave a secret message to track down a Wild Thing. Or, maybe if you leave a secret message, one will get in touch.

Design a secret code

Invent a secret code to send messages to your friends. You could flash a mirror, bang sticks on a tree trunk, beat a drum or blow a stick whistle. Maybe try Morse code, which represents letters using combinations of long and short sounds.

Morse code		
A •—	J •———	S •••
B —•••	K —•—	T —
C —•—•	L •—••	U ••—
D —••	M ——	V •••—
E •	N —•	W •——
F ••—•	O ———	X —••—
G ——•	P •——•	Y —•——
H ••••	Q ——•—	Z ——••
I ••	R •—•	

Can you decode this message?

Make a wild drum

Ancient communities would beat rhythms on drums to send messages and warnings through the forest or over the mountains. Make up your own sound patterns to pass on messages when hunting for Wild Things, perhaps using long and short notes like Morse code.

You will need:
An old biscuit tin, double-sided tape, leaves, a long bendy creeper stem and two strong sticks.

1. Stick bands of tape around the tin and decorate with leaves.

2. Tie creeper around the tin in rings, making one piece into a long handle so you can hang the drum around your neck.

3. Choose two strong straight sticks to be your drumsticks.

4. Agree on a secret code with your friends, then take your drum into the woods and beat out a message. Can your friends understand it?

Invisible inks and messages

Try some of these different ways to write a secret message for your friends' eyes only – perhaps directions to a hidden meeting place or clues to find treasure.

You will need:

Bicarbonate of soda, water, lemon juice, wild berry ink (see page 45), a paint brush and paper.

Secret ink

Mix bicarbonate of soda with water in equal parts. Paint a message onto a piece of paper with the mixture and let it dry. To reveal the message, paint over it with wild berry ink or lemon juice.

Secret ink

Berry ink

Write your message in code.

Secret alphabets and codes

To make your secret message even more secure from prying eyes, you could invent your own alphabet.

Magic runes

This alphabet of symbols is based on ancient Viking runes, the perfect way to send magical messages to other Wild Thing explorers. Can you decipher the message?

Sending messages in code

Try different wild ways to send messages, such as writing with a stick in mud, sand or snow. This message says 'follow the stream to the first house'.

Lesson 7:
Magic spells and potions

Have you ever wanted to become invisible or transform your best friend into a snail? Would you like to shrink to the size of a fairy, or change your dog into a unicorn? It's time to practise your magic!

Magic herbs

Dandelion tonic

Mermaid sponge

Dragon eyeballs

Feather quills

Goblin toenails

Villenass
16 09

Fairy wishes

Troll backscratchers

Wizard's blackberry go-faster potion

Mermaid's false fingernails

Elderberry potion

Dragon's blood

Rosehip potion

Magical spell cabinet

Whatever the weather and the time of year, always carry some bags and containers with you so you can gather magical ingredients for spells and potions. You'll also need a special place to keep your wild collection until you're ready to make some magic. Transform an old cupboard or some spare shelves into a secret spell cabinet, just like this one.

Troll nose hair

Goblin snot

Safety tips
• Don't collect poisonous berries and leaves.
• Don't eat any of your spell cabinet ingredients.
• Some materials should only be kept for a short while. If in doubt ask a grown-up.

Magic lamp (does it contain a genie?)

Evil monster's eyeballs

Elderflower shrinking potion

Dragon eggs and goblin treats

Potion of peppermint

Magic ink

Troll toothpicks

Spell ingredients

Spells need ingredients with powers specially chosen by you. Here are a few ideas to get you started.

Cornflour mixture

Or troll snot for gloopy spells (see page 165)

Moss clumps

Witch's or goblin's warts, perfect for gruesome spells

Early morning dew

A popular ingredient in many spells

Cherry blossom

Adds colour and perfume to fairy spells

Egg shells

A discarded dragon egg is essential for bad spells

Preserved raven skull

This rare witch's ingredient should be used wisely

Sea-polished stones and shells

These mermaid jewels will double the magic of your spell

Dandelion seeds

These fairy wishes are perfect for charms

Snail shells

These troll snacks will pack a punch

Dried flaky leaves

Troll fingernails for a scratchy itchy spell

Fairy hoar frost

Looks like frozen jewels

Honesty seed cases

Great for truth serums and lie detector spells

Spell magic

To get a spell to work, you don't just need the right ingredients. You also need to make sure you do the magic in the right way.

Choose a magical place. Spells won't work if you're sitting indoors in front of the TV. Go outside and find a magic spot, fine-tune your wild senses and feel the power of nature.

Find the right wild words to conjure up magic, bring wild places alive and inspire stories and dreams.

Learn the power of wild ingredients, such as using a winged seed for flight or a dewdrop for clear sight.

Get the right equipment. A special container, perhaps a clay jar, a metal cauldron or a magic bottle, is best for brewing spells.

Pick the right wand. Is it a fairy's spell or a witch's spell?

Channel your energy to become part of the spell. You might close your eyes, spin around, dance and direct energy through your wand.

Learn to make magical wands on pages 70 & 94.

Making spells

Each spell is personal to whoever creates it, but here are a few ideas to get you started – just add your own magic. Experiment until you make the perfect spell, then record it in your spell book (see page 44).

Fairy attraction spell

Pour freshly collected rainwater into a magic bottle. Add a few ingredients – maybe a rush of wind, a pinch of cherry blossom, a drop of spring dew, and tiny flower petals. If you mix in a little gelatin with the water, the petals will float. Dab some of the mixture on your wrists like perfume and then hide the bottle among plants with a mini-wand as a fairy gift (see page 94). What will happen next?

Troll protection spell

Tie together a snail shell (guaranteed to tempt a troll), some honesty seeds and sweet-smelling herbs (to stop them telling lies and playing tricks) and a blackthorn spike (to pin them to the spot until the sun comes up and turns them to stone). What other ideas can you come up with?

Bad spells

The perfect ingredients for a bad spell might include:

- Green troll nasal hair and toothpicks
- Goblin snot
- A dragon's egg shell
- A raven's skull
- An icy breath of wind

Find a dark cave, a damp mossy hollow or a hollow tree and weave a spell.

A spell is like a recipe – first you need to gather your ingredients together.

Green troll nasal hair

40

Love spell

To fall deeply in love with the wild world, go to a beautiful wild place, smell some petal perfume, listen to the birds singing and find the softest velvety moss pillow you can. Lie down and shut your eyes. What can you smell, what can you feel, what can you hear?

Safety tip
• Remember – magic spells are never eaten!
• Always wash your hands after handling wild spell ingredients.

Troll toothpick

Dried goblin snot

Magic potions

Put your foraging skills to the test (see page 18) by collecting fresh edible ingredients. Be sure to get a grown-up to help. Mix the ingredients together to make tasty potions. Some are especially delicious poured over ice cream! You could make potions for Wild Thing superpowers – would you like to see like an owl, hear like a bat or climb like a lizard?

You will need:

Berries and herbs, sugar, water, saucepans, a sieve, little bottles and labels.

1. Collect edible berries and herbs in separate containers. Be sure you know what you are collecting.
2. Wash them in clean, cold water.

A magic potion collection

Create a range of magic potions for every occasion – to help bring you luck, to make you feel braver, to shrink you down to the size of an ant, or anything else you want.

Dragon's blood – lucky potion

Mint imagination potion

Elderberry superpower energy potion

3. Prepare your ingredients:

Berries – use a spoon to mash them in a bowl, then squeeze through a sieve or a pair of tights to make a smooth potion.

Fruits – some fruits may need to be gently simmered in a saucepan with a little sugar.

Rosehips – leave them whole and pour boiling water over them, then leave to cool.

Herbs – remove the leaves, mix with hot water and leave to cool.

4. Put each potion in a clean bottle or jar. Label each one with a name and a superpower.

5. Refrigerate and eat (or drink) within a few days.

Safety tips
• Be very careful to choose fresh edible berries and flowers. If in any doubt, don't eat/drink your potions.

Blackberry wizard's black magic potion

Dandelion bravery potion

Elderflower shrinking potion

Rosehip protection potion

Wild damson wind power potion

Lesson 8:

Make a magical spell book

Be sure to note down all your best spells so you can summon their power again. For an extra touch of magic, write your spells in a beautiful spell book in secret code with wild ink.

Make a magic spell book

You will need:

Special paper, raffia or string, a tea bag and wild materials.

1. Find some special paper, such as thick watercolour paper, handmade paper or natural paper made of a thin piece of flaky bark.

2. To make the paper look ancient and mysterious, dunk a tea bag in a small amount of hot water, let it cool and then drag it over the paper.

3. Once the paper has dried, fold several sheets to make a little book. Tie raffia or string around the fold, then add some special decoration, perhaps a magic feather and an elf's acorn helmet.

Wild ink

Have fun making wild colours when fruits and nuts ripen in the autumn. For each recipe, boil the mixture in a saucepan for a few minutes. Let the mixture cool before sieving it into a bowl to make a smooth ink. Store your ink in labelled bottles. Remember, it doesn't keep for long.

You will need:
Wild fruits, nuts and galls, salt, vinegar, old nails, old saucepan, jar, sieve, pestle and mortar.

Oak gall ink

For yellowy brown ink, put a few old iron nails in a jar of rainwater and leave outside to rust for about a week. Collect a handful of galls from an oak tree, pound in a pestle and mortar, and then put them in an old saucepan with 1 cup of strained iron water and 1 teaspoon of salt.

Berry ink

To make pinky-purple ink, put half a cup of berries, half a teaspoon of vinegar (to hold the colour) and half a teaspoon of salt (as a preservative) in a saucepan. Try different berries to see how many different colours you can make.

Walnut ink

For dark brown ink, put 3–4 green outer walnut husks in an old saucepan with 1 teaspoon each of salt and vinegar, and 1 cup of water.

Walnut ink

Berry ink

Oak gall ink

Experiment with other wild materials to make other colours, such as huckleberries (denim blue), charcoal (black) and sloe berries (dark purply blue).

Magic pencil

Don't use any old pencil to write down your spells. A wild magic pencil always works better! Use a wood with a pithy core, such as elder.

You will need:

A pencil length of freshly cut wood, a skewer, a knife, charcoal, ribbons, wool and feathers.

1. Scrape the bark off your stick, then use the skewer to scrape out the pith at one end. If not using elder, you may need to use a knife to carve a hole in the wood.

2. Push one end of a thin piece of charcoal into the hole in the stick.

3. Decorate with feathers and ribbons – white feathers for good spells and black for more sinister ones!

Magic quill

Write your spells with a magic feather – the grander the feather, the more powerful the spell!

You will need:
Large strong feathers and a sharp knife.

1. Shave off some of the barbs at the lower end of the feather with a knife.

2. Cut the end of the quill to a point.

3. Dip the tip of the quill in your wild ink and start writing!

Safety tip
• Be very careful when using sharp knives.
• Always get a grown-up to help.

The Wild Things and their worlds

The **Wild Things** of fairy tales and legends fill our imaginations. But now it's time to get out there and meet them for real. So, turn the pages to start discovering the magical worlds of dragons, witches, wizards, elves, fairies, monsters, mermaids, giants, unicorns, goblins, trolls and who knows what else…

Dragons

Just because you've never seen a dragon, that doesn't mean they don't exist. Like many wild creatures, dragons can be shy and secretive, and may only come out at night when you're tucked up in bed. But get outside with your wild skills at the ready, because you never know what you might find.

Dragons can be gigantic or tiny, terrifying or friendly. Some may be your enemy but, if you're very lucky, others may befriend you, protecting you and sharing their magic powers.

Dragons live in wild places everywhere, from the highest mountains and darkest caves to the wildest forest. They may even be hiding among the trees at your local park. So be brave, get out there, and get dragon hunting!

How to track a dragon

The wild world is full of scaly surprises. Look carefully and you will discover evidence of dragons everywhere. Here are some top dragon clues to look out for.

Skin and scales

Just like snakes, every time a dragon grows a bit bigger, it sheds its outer layer of skin. Search for thick, wrinkly skin, or for leafy, spiky or spotty scales.

Dragon eggs

Some eggs are green and camouflaged, others are pink and spiky. They can also look like birds eggs – perhaps a baby dragon has just hatched from a broken egg shell?

Claws and claw marks

Can you spot where a dragon has sharpened its long claws on a tree trunk? Look out for lost claw tips.

Horns

These can be lost in a fight, and may be rough and woody or green and spiky.

Signs of fire

Dragons can be careless with their fiery breath — look for burnt charcoal or charred bits of wood.

Wings

Most dragons have bat-like wings with thin skin stretched between long bones, but others have feathery wings. So be sure to hunt for both wing fronds and big feathers.

Dragon pathways

Search for snapped twigs, sticks or even branches (depending on the size of your dragon!) or hunt for dragon tracks in the mud, snow or sand. Are you brave enough to follow their footprints?

Teeth

Sometimes lost at meal times, dragons' big gnarly teeth can look like sharp stones.

Dragon's lair

Dragons sleep in dark, damp, hidden places — perhaps a cave's entrance, an underground hidey hole, among an old tree's twisted roots or inside a hollow tree.

53

Discovering hidden dragons

Dragons are very good at not being seen. But every now and then you may catch a glimpse of one. Can you take a dragon by surprise, seeing through its cunning disguises?

Head out to the woods, the park or the beach. How many cleverly camouflaged dragons can you spot?

Can you see the giant dragon eye? Try looking through half-closed eyes.

Are you brave enough to climb inside a dragon's belly and have a picnic? Or perhaps you could scramble along its long knobbly tail, or maybe even take a ride on its back.

You can hunt for the bones and skeletons of dead dragons. They may be disguised as tree trunks or rocks. Did they fall in battle with other dragons or were they turned to wood or stone by a wicked witch?

Use wild materials to reveal hidden dragons — you might add bright eyes, big ears, fierce teeth, feathery wings and big claws.

Leave your dragon for future adventures or for other dragon hunters to discover.

Snow and ice dragons

Some cunning dragons use magic to make themselves invisible. But freezing weather can break the spell, revealing their true form to sharp-eyed dragon spotters.

Hunt for clues in ice and snow. Keep an eye out for...

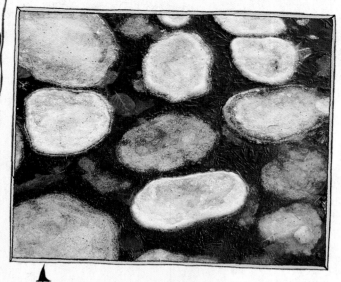

Dragon scales floating on frozen rivers

Dragon spines hidden among frosty plants

Dragon backbones emerging from a frozen landscape

A miniature ice dragon peering out from a frozen waterfall

Safety tip
• Always have an adult with you when exploring near water.

Making a snow dragon

Use wintry materials to make a friend for all the ice and snow dragons.

You will need:
A large plastic box, a trowel and some broken ice from a frozen puddle.

1. Pack snow into the plastic box to make building blocks.
2. Use the snow blocks to make a long dragon's body and tail.
3. Fill in the gaps with fresh snow and carve details with the trowel.
4. Make a big head with a gaping mouth and sharp icy teeth.
5. Add spines of snow or ice all along the body and tail.

How scary is your snow dragon?

Bottle magic dragon breath

Ice dragons breathe frost instead of fire. You may not see them but perhaps you can capture some of their icy breath and borrow some of their magic power.

You will need:
A special bottle and a magic label.

1. Go outside on a cold day when your breath forms clouds in the air.
2. Breathe heavily into the bottle to capture the chilly dragon breath.
3. Put the top on quickly!
4. Add a label and store in a freezer until you are ready to go on a quest – the magic dragon breath should protect you from unfriendly dragons.

57

Dragonflies

These dragons once flew around with the dinosaurs. To discover underwater dragonfly nymphs, go to a pond or stream and drag a net or a sieve through the water. Tip your catch into a container of water to see if you have caught a young underwater dragon.

Nature's dragons

The real dragons of the natural world may be small and not breathe fire, but they've been around for millions of years and have developed amazing magical powers.

Where to look: near rivers and ponds

Magic powers

Dragonflies spend up to five years as underwater nymphs, gobbling up tadpoles, insects and baby fish. Then one summer day, the nymph emerges onto a leaf, sits in the sun and transforms into a beautiful winged adult.

Safety tip
• Always have an adult with you when exploring near water or old walls.

Newts

Look for these dragon-like amphibians in ponds and ditches during the spring. At other times, they hang out in damp places in woods, parks and gardens. They eat underwater creatures and also gobble up worms and beetles. You can catch newts with a net or a sieve, but treat them very carefully and always return them to their home.

Where to look: near rivers and ponds

Magic powers

If they lose their tail or a leg, newts can just regrow a new one! They hibernate in cold weather, sometimes underwater.

Where to look: dry places, stone walls, heathland and rough grassland

Lizards

These prehistoric-looking reptiles can often be seen in the summer months, sunbathing or scuttling across rocks.

Magic powers
A group of lizards called chameleons can change their skin colour to match their surroundings or to signal to one another. Other lizards can regrow a lost tail.

Dragon nests

Just like birds, dragons need to hide and protect their eggs and young in carefully built nests.

What sort of nest does your dragon need? Here are a few ideas…

For a large dragon, weave tree branches and sticks together to make a nest fit for an enormous egg. You can decorate it with leaves for camouflage.

If your dragon is pocket-sized (and some of the fiercest ones are), make a nest inspired by birds, using twigs, grasses and leaves. Don't line it with soft moss and feathers; dragons prefer prickly leaves and thorns.

Dragon eggs

Have you ever dreamt of having your own pet dragon? Follow these steps to design a magical dragon egg.

You will need:
Cones, pebbles or potatoes, clay, seeds, leaves and petals.

1. Collect egg-shaped objects, such as fir cones or pebbles, or ask an adult for some large potatoes from the kitchen. Cover each "egg" in a layer of clay, at least 0.5 cm (¼ in) thick. Smooth the clay with your fingertips.

2. Now it's time to decorate. Gather some wild materials and press them into the clay to make each of your eggs unique. How will your eggs reflect the personalities of the dragons inside? A beautiful brightly coloured egg may hatch into a friendly dragon, or a scaly camouflaged egg covered in spikes and thorns might become a fierce one.

3. Place the eggs carefully in a dragon nest and wait for the hatchling to emerge!

Baby dragons

When your egg hatches, what will your baby dragon (or dragons) look like?

You will need:

Dragon sticks, clay and lots of loose wild materials.

1. Choose a dragon stick. Pick one that's a bit crooked with rough bark, or maybe a forked stick for a dragon with horns – or even a two-headed dragon!

2. Wrap a lump of clay securely around one end of the stick; moulding it into a dragon's head.

3. What sort of dragon will you make? Bring it to life with a magic spell, adding wild materials to make big staring eyes, long ears or horns, tough scales and sharp teeth. You may also wish to add a body with wings – it's up to you.

4. Now your dragon puppet is ready for a dragon drama in an outdoor puppet show. Add to the drama by making other Wild Things, such as a witch or a fairy.

Defending your dragon

Once you've befriended a wild dragon, get ready to defend it from whatever enemies might be out there – and to protect its precious hoard of hidden treasure.

You will need:

A pen knife, modelling balloons, string, cardboard or hardboard, and some paint.

Sword

Find a strong straight stick. Carefully scrape off the bark with a knife and whittle the wood into a sword shape, making sure the tip is blunt. Use the sword as it is, or make a handle:

If your stick is bendy, bend one end round and tie in place to make a curved handle, like this.

To make a straight handle, bind two strong twigs together around one end of your sword with string, like this.

Catapult

First choose a strong Y-shaped stick. Tie a long stretchy modelling balloon between the arms of the Y.

← Use soft ammunition like these flour bombs, made by wrapping a spoonful of flour tightly in a sheet of kitchen roll.

Shield

Even the bravest dragon warrior needs protection. Cut out a shield shape from firm cardboard or hardboard. Stick a handle on the back with hot glue. Paint your shield with a coat of arms to show you are a heroic dragon defender.

Safety tips
- Take care when using knives – ask for a grown-up's help.
- Don't point sticks or fire catapults at people or animals.
- Hot-glue guns should only be used under close supervision.

Dragon's blood

Dragon's blood is said to have special magical powers, offering protection from all unfriendly Wild Things. Would your dragon be willing to share a few drops of its blood in exchange for your friendship?

Edible berries

You will need:

Edible berries (check with someone who knows which ones are good to eat), sugar, a saucepan, a sieve, a funnel, and a special bottle with a magic label.

Straining the berries

Making special dragon's blood

This activity should be done in the autumn when wild berries are growing.

1. Go to a wild place to gather edible berries, such as damsons, elderberries or blackberries.
2. Take some berries home to stew in a saucepan with a little water and some sugar. Experiment with different berries to find the right colour.
3. Let the mixture cool, then strain it through a sieve to make smooth, gloopy dragon's blood.
4. Pour it through a funnel into your bottle.
5. Trickle the blood over ice cream for a magical treat – it will give you an energy boost and protect you from unfriendly dragons.

Safety tip
• Make sure you only collect edible berries. Always check with an adult who knows which are safe to eat.

Dragon's blood

The finished product!

Wands

Witches and wizards

You probably know that witches and wizards are good at magic, casting spells and generally being a bit scary. But did you also know about their close connection with nature and wild places? They create most of their magic using wild plants and animals, which gives them a deep understanding of the natural world.

Discover how witches and wizards utilize nature's power, and have fun making magic costumes, broomsticks and spooky haunts in the woods.

Pets Corner

Witch and wizard costumes

Use these wild witch and wizard costumes immediately, before the wild colours fade.

You will need:
Stiff black paper, scissors, double-sided tape, pencil, glue, wool, wild leaves and feathers.

Witches' and wizards' hats

1. Cut a semicircle from a large sheet of black paper, then fold it into a cone big enough to fit on your head. Tape the sides of the cone to secure in place.

2. Draw around a medium-sized plate on black paper and cut out the circle.

Leaf shapes

Collect yellowing autumn leaves, and cut them into moons, scary faces, lightning bolts and stars. To make a leaf star, fold a leaf in half and then in quarters. Cut as shown and then open out to reveal a star shape.

3. To make the hat's rim, place the base of the cone in the middle of the paper circle and draw round it.

4. Mark and cut lines from the centre to the edge of the circle you just drew, making a series of triangles. Fold the triangles up and stick them inside the cone hat to create a strong rim.

5. Decorate the hat with stars and feathers, sticking them on with double-sided tape or glue.

• Alternatively, you could buy a hat and decorate that.

Wizards' and witches' cloaks

Make amazing magical cloaks from black fabric decorated with an assortment of colourful autumn leaves or leaf shapes stuck on with double-sided tape or glue.

Magic sticks

Go outside in search of magic sticks. You may think that all sticks are just ordinary sticks, but look carefully and you will find one perfect for a speedy broomstick, a powerful wizard's staff or a wild witch's wand.

Make a magic broomstick

A witch or wizard broomstick can take you on all sorts of adventures, but how do you add the magic that transforms an ordinary looking bit of wood into a magical broomstick?

You will need:
A large stick, lots of smaller twigs, string and paint.

1. Carefully choose a magic stick (or does it choose you?). The stick should be strong and sturdy but have something special about it. Perhaps it has a section that is comfortable to sit on and could be made into a seat, or maybe it has a handle shaped like a monster's head.

2. Collect a large bunch of twigs. Arrange some twigs around one end of the broomstick, tying them on firmly with string. Then arrange the rest of the twigs around the first bunch and tie them on firmly too.

3. Paint your broom to increase its magic. You may want go-faster stripes, a mystical pattern or, if it has a knobbly end, you could turn it into a scary head or a control panel.

Make a magic witch or wizard wand

If you want to turn your sister green or make your brother disappear, you'll need your own wand. First, find a stick that feels right in your hand — each type of wood has different magical qualities — then decorate it with special wild materials that mean something to you.

Add magic to your wand by scraping off the bark and sticking on wild materials or by whittling, painting and polishing. The more you work on your wand, the more magic it will hold, and the more personal it will be to you. Here are a few wild wand ideas:

You will need:

A stick, double-sided tape, glue or clay, paints and wild materials.

Wrap double-sided tape around your wand. Stick on magical wild materials: perhaps feathers for flight, shells for protection, lichen for magic growing power or a sprig of wild herbs to keep you healthy.

Use a wood-burning (or 'pyrography') tool to burn patterns or animal pictures into the wood.

A wand doesn't have to be straight. Try a curvy wand with a magical handle bound with twine.

Paint your wand to match your broomstick. Perhaps this will make them both more powerful.

You could add feathers, shells and even a bleached bird's skull to ward off evil magic.

When you invite your witch and wizard friends around, insist they all put their wands in a pot so nobody casts a spell by mistake!

Make a wizard's staff

Wands are good for small-scale magic, but if you want to try out some BIG spells or compete with other wizards, you'll need a much more powerful staff. Choose a large sturdy stick that is almost as tall as you. The magical monster staff on the right has a collar decorated with thorns, a fluffy beard, shell and acorn eyes, feathers for hair and a spiky conker headdress.

Sea wizards

To make a beach staff for a sea wizard, hunt for driftwood, pounded and shaped by the sea to give it extra magic. Decorate with shells, sea-washed glass, feathers and seaweed.

The amulet around this staff's neck contains a magic spell written on birch bark paper (see page 77).

Safety tips
• Take care when using knives or wood-burning tools! Ask for a grown-up's help.

Witch and wizard pets

Witches and wizards have a magical way with wild creatures, which can be their trusted companions, magical assistants and helpful spies. They favour owls, ravens, mice, bats, spiders, snakes and the domestic cat.

You will need:

Odd old socks, newspaper, string, a hot-glue gun, wild materials, including fir cones, feathers, leaves and clay.

A friendly owl, sure to be a loyal friend and a reliable sender of messages.

Make a witch's owl or a wizard's raven

Use a few simple materials to make your own witch or wizard pet.

1. Choose a sock. This would usually be black for a raven or brown for an owl. But you could make a red raven or a pink owl – this is your special magical pet!

2. Stuff the sock with scrunched up newspaper.

3. Use a glue gun to stick wild materials, such as feather wings, stick feet, a leaf face, seed features and whatever else you might have to bring your pet alive.

4. Attach a length of string so you can hang up your bird or make it fly.

Safety tip
• Hot-glue guns should only be used under close adult supervision!

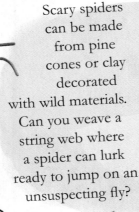

Other pet ideas

You can create other pets from stuffed socks, like this magical bird made with leaves stuck on cardboard wings, twiggy feet and a feather tail, all ready to hang from your broom.

Scary spiders can be made from pine cones or clay decorated with wild materials. Can you weave a string web where a spider can lurk ready to jump on an unsuspecting fly?

Cut out bat shapes from large leaves, or make a fir-cone bat with a clay head, seed eyes and leafy wings.

Secrets of the wild

Aim to become more like a witch or wizard, using all your wild skills to spy on wild creatures and discover some of their secrets. Look out for their nests, their tracks or for other clues they leave behind — an owl pellet, a raven's feather, a nut chewed by a mouse. And remember that wild creatures also spy on you, watching your every move…

Witch and wizard haunts

It's no good practising your magic in your bedroom. You need to get outside and find a wild hidey hole to transform into a magical haunt, somewhere to hang out with your witch and wizard friends – like the one on pages 64–65. Look for an old tree, a fallen tree trunk, an abandoned den in the woods, or a secret area at the bottom of the garden. Transform it into a spooky place to brew potions and practise magic spells. For a really wild experience, visit your haunt after dark with magical lanterns (see Magic lanterns, page 167).

A few haunting ideas:

Make a place to sit. It could be a tree throne surrounded by twisted roots or a log stool handy for stirring up spells in the cauldron.

For something really scary, use a bleached skull lantern with eye sockets lit by night lights.

Safety tip
• Never leave lit night lights unattended.
• Always wash hands carefully after handling bones.

Find a level spot for your cauldron so you can mix spells without spilling any magic.

Find nooks and crannies to store your spell bottles and magic ingredients.

Add jar lanterns decorated with spooky leaf faces tucked under an elastic band.

Make a mini-witch or wizard

Make a little magical friend to protect your haunt when you aren't there.

You will need:

A stick, clay, a little hat, an elastic band and some wild materials.

1. Put a fist full of clay on one end of the stick, and mould it into a scary face.

2. Add wild grassy hair, scary eyes, stone or stick teeth and whatever else you can think of to make a scary-looking witch or wizard.

3. Make a small hat (a mini version of your own hat, see page 66) and dress him or her in a leafy cape attached with string or an elastic band.

Autumnal leaves make a great red and golden leafy cloak.

Make a spell bottle

This little bottle is a lucky charm, filled with tiny wild materials to protect you from unfriendly witches and wizards.

You will need:
A tiny bottle with a well-fitting lid, a leather cord or some string.

1. Go on a witch scavenger hunt in the woods or at the park. You might find a feather (from the breast of a wizard's raven), a snail shell (for protection), a red berry (for blood), some fluffy seeds (a dragon's ear hair) and a tiny acorn (a Wild Thing's eyeball). How many tiny magical materials can you fit inside your bottle?

This isn't a wild magical thing, it's just a safety pin so you can see how tiny the other things are.

2. Find a piece of papery birch bark or make some magic paper (see page 44). Write a magical spell for your wild ingredients.

3. Fill the bottle and put the top on tight so no magic can escape!

Try to find a bottle with a cork stopper for a lid.

Cauldrons

Discover spooky natural cauldrons out in the wilds where a witch or a wizard might stir up powerful spells.

Wild magic

Find your own mossy cauldron, add a little extra water and some magical ingredients (maybe some used fairy wings, an elf's cup and a dragon's scale) and stir up a muddy spell with a mixing stick or a magic wand.

Moss cauldrons

Witches and wizards often use natural cauldrons, like this hollow tree stump where water has collected.

For extra magical protection, surround the cauldron with sticks, feathers, bleached bones or other wild treasures.

To conjure up good spells, add some colourful leaves, like this autumn cauldron saying farewell to long sunny days before the long dark nights of winter.

Brew up a fizzy spell

Witches and wizards are experts at brewing up strange concoctions. Become a wild scientist with a bubbling outdoor cauldron experiment. This green mixture may look evil but perhaps it will bring you good luck!

You will need: A metal cauldron (a cast iron pot or an old saucepan), vinegar, bicarbonate of soda, food colouring, water and wild ingredients from your spell cabinet (see pages 36–37).

1. The best spells are always the messiest ones, so take the cauldron outside.

2. Add wild ingredients. This cauldron contains heather for luck, dandelion wishes, rosehips for health, and spiky hairs from a wizard's beard for long life.

3. Pour water and vinegar into the cauldron with some natural food colouring.

4. Now for the magic! Add a spoonful of bicarbonate of soda – the mixture will bubble and fizz, releasing the spell's magic into the air (or, more scientifically, the reaction releases carbon dioxide gas).

5. Stir with a stick or an old wooden spoon and release the magic with a tap of your wand.

6. Experiment with different quantities of vinegar and baking soda. What happens when you add washing-up liquid or use warm water?

Elves and fairies

Fairies and elves are small creatures who live in woods and meadows, city parks or gardens and among the pots on patios and balconies. Like all Wild Things, they draw their energy and magic from nature – so don't be tempted to keep them indoors or make them anything from plastic! They belong in nature, among their beautiful friends: the butterflies, bees, moths, lacewings, bugs and beetles.

Get outside anywhere and at any time of year in search of these little Wild Things, but remember, they only trust true fairy friends. Look out for fairies in the dew on a spider's web, floating in sunbeams, or find natural fairy glitter in frost and snow (the only kind of glitter that real fairies like!). You can also gather together wild materials and take them home to make your own fairies and elves to release later.

Are there *fairies* at the bottom of the garden?

Of course there are! But only true fairy-believers can spot them. Become a mini-detective and use your wild skills to go on a scavenger hunt, looking for clues from the world of fairies and elves. You can do this in every season and even after dark. Look out for…

An elf's kit bag

This elf's leafy kit bag contains a snail-shell water bottle, an acorn cup, a rope of woven grass, a flint fire lighter (there are no matches in the fairy world), a beech nut snack, a woolly blanket for keeping warm, chalk, and a roll of birch bark paper for writing secret messages.

An elf's catapult

Little people can be very careless and leave things behind, such as this tiny catapult made from a twig.

Fairy wings

The wings of fairies wear out and need replacing in the same way birds' feathers do. Look out for a frost fairy's discarded glittery wings or an autumn fairy's multicoloured wings.

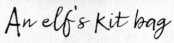

Fairy and elf homes and gardens

Can you spot clues to where they live, such as hidden doorways and windows, tiny mossy gardens or little swimming pools hidden among roots or branches?

Leave a message for the fairies and elves

Fairies and elves are very shy but a secret message may draw them out.

1. Write a message with a magic pen on papery bark or magic paper (see pages 44–45) in secret ink.

2. Roll up the paper and push it into a little bottle.

3. Leave the bottle somewhere outdoors where fairies may be hiding. Check it after a few days to see if you have had a reply!

4. Be sure to take the bottle home with you after checking it.

You will need:
A magic pen, thin bark or paper and a small bottle.

To the fairies, TOP SECRET!

Mum and Dad say fairies aren't real, but I'm sure you are out there. Please reply so I can prove them wrong! PS I don't have any wobbly teeth just now, is there anything else you would like? Chocolate?

83

Making flower fairies and leaf elves

If you can't find any fairies or elves, create your own using common flowers and petals, green leaves and seeds.

You will need:
Fishing line, florist's wire, berries, leaves and petals, double-sided sticky tape.

1. Bend the end of an 8 cm (3 in) length of florist's wire to make a loop.

2. Choose a flower hat and thread it along the wire until it is next to the loop.

3. Find a berry for the head. Thread it along the wire, followed by stem arms with buds or seeds for hands.

4. Add a flower body followed by a flower skirt (and legs) or trousers.

Flower fairies

Flower fairies fade fast, so make the most of them while you can. Hang them outside your window or use them as tree or party decorations.

5. Bend the bottom of the wire to hold everything in place. Stick on petal or leaf wings with double-sided tape.

6. Thread transparent fishing line through the loop so you can carry your fairy around with you.

Leaf elves

To make a leaf elf, thread leaves and buds onto wire. This elf has leafy armour, a belt with a berry buckle, and a bud head with fluffy ears.

Home in a jar

Keep your fairy safe by making a beautiful, flowery home.

You will need:

A glass jar, moss, feathers, blossoms, fairy dust, an elastic band and sticky tape.

1. Tape the fishing line onto the lid so the fairy can stand up in the jar.

2. Line the bottom of the jar with moss, fairy treasures and a sprinkle of fairy dust (see page 93).

3. Place the lid on the jar and wrap an elastic band around it.

4. Make your jar fit for a fairy, by tucking feathers, blossoms and other decorations around the lid.

85

Flower-fairy badges

Wearing a flower-fairy badge is a way of showing fairies that you are their friend, so they are less likely to hide from you.

You will need:

Thin cardboard, safety pins, double-sided tape, leaves, feathers and petals.

Use colourful petals from lots of different flowers.

1. Cut the card into the shape of a body and head, then cover one side of the body with double-sided tape.

2. Draw a face on the front of the head and tape a safety pin to the back of it.

3. Tape some wings – perhaps leaves, feathers or petals – onto the fairy's back.

4. Create a wonderful outfit by adding colourful petals to the tape on the front.

Wild elf challenge

Not all magical creatures need to be carefully made at home. On an adventure, quickly create some elves and fairies using wild materials and clay.

You will need:

Clay, wild materials (such as sticks, nuts, seeds, flower petals, empty snail shells and feathers), raffia or string, a pen knife and scissors.

1. Can you find a small stick with arms and legs? If not, you may need to tie some on with string.

2. Wrap some clay around one end of the stick to make the head. Or you may prefer to carve a little face in the wood with a pen knife.

3. Add feathers, seeds, leaves, flowers and other wild materials to make clothes and wings, sticking them on with clay, or using raffia or string.

4. Be sure to use whatever material you can find. So, for a beach elf, you could use driftwood decorated with seaweed and shells.

Safety tip
• Only use a knife with grown-up help.

Fairy fashions

Every fairy dreams of having a wardrobe full of stunning outfits, ready to dress up for all the fairy parties.

Make a cardboard cutout fairy

First, you need a model for all the great fairy fashions you're going to create.

You will need:
White cardboard, double-sided tape, hook-and-loop sticky pads, scissors and a collection of wild materials.

1. Draw a fairy doll on white card, standing on a base. This doll should be about 15 cm (6 in) tall.

2. Cut out the fairy, then cut a slit in the base. Cut a rectangle of card the same size as the base, which can be slotted in to the base at a right angle to make the doll stand up.

3. Draw a face on your fairy and paint the body and base if you wish.

4. Stick a few small sticky pads onto the front of the fairy doll, and one on the rear, so you can attach clothes to the front and wings to the back.

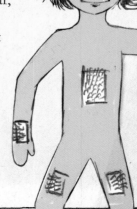

5. Cut out cardboard wings, dresses and hats. Put sticky pads on one side so you can stick them to the fairy. Cover the other side with double-sided tape.

Wings

Hat

Dresses

6. Attach leaves, petals, seeds or feathers to the double-sided tape on the cardboard pieces to make whatever outfit fairies are wearing this season.

Be very careful when attaching petals. You don't want your fairy to end up with a torn dress!

89

Design seasonal fairy fashions

Gather wild materials to design an outfit for your fairy
that's perfectly suited to the current season.

Yellow flowers are a spring favourite

Spring collection

Look for bright green leaves, fallen spring flowers and fruit blossom.

Try a sleeveless number for the perfect summer dress

Pink is a must for the hotter months

Summer collection

Gather some of summer's bright fallen petals.

Acorn cups make perfect hats

A mini feather lifts any autumnal hat

Autumn's the time for a saw toothed hem

Autumn collection

Be inspired by yellow, orange, red and golden leaves falling from the trees.

Fern fronds make a real statement

Winter collection

Even in winter, you can find beautiful materials for fairy fashions. Look for:
feathers, seeds, and dried and evergreen leaves.

Fairy and elf magic

Fairies and elves use flower-power to weave their magic spells. Flowers have amazing magical properties. Their bright colours and sweet scents attract flying insects to crawl among their petals and gorge on sugary nectar and pollen. The insects then take the pollen to other flowers, helping them make seeds and grow in new places.

Make magic petal confetti

Scatter magic petals in the air to make fairy wishes or use it to create magic fairy dust.

You will need:

Kitchen roll, a tray and petals.

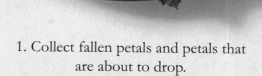

Fairy perfume

Make a beautiful scented fairy perfume.

You will need:

Flowers, petals, herb leaves and a small glass.

1. Gather sweet-smelling flowers and herb leaves.

2. Arrange them in a glass of water decorated with flower parasols.

1. Collect fallen petals and petals that are about to drop.

2. Spread the petals out on absorbent kitchen roll on a tray, then put them somewhere warm (such as an airing cupboard) until the petals are completely dry.

3. Store the petal confetti in an open container until you are ready to use it.

Dandelion wishes

Blowing on a dandelion's fluffy seed head releases beautiful floating fairy wishes (or are they fairies?).

You will need:
Dandelion seed heads, a jar and wishes.

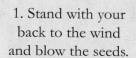

1. Stand with your back to the wind and blow the seeds.

2. Make a wish as you watch the seeds float away.

3. If you would like a store of wishes to share with friends, collect some dandelion seed heads and keep them in a jar in your spell cabinet.

Magic fairy dust

Blowing a little fairy dust into the air may make your fairy dreams and wishes come true!

You will need:
Salt, food colouring, petals or petal confetti.

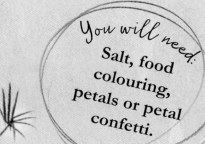

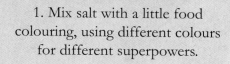

1. Mix salt with a little food colouring, using different colours for different superpowers.

2. Add fresh or dried petals (or petal confetti) and mix well to make a colourful mixture.

3. Take fairy dust on all your fairy adventures.

Wands

Wild magical wands are perfect for showering all kinds of spells. Make teeny-weeny ones for real fairies and larger ones for you and your friends.

Wands for your friends

Choose larger sticks that feel magical when you hold them. You could peel the bark off and smooth the wand with sandpaper.

Real fairy wands

Store tiny wands in a little bottle, to take out on fairy adventures and give to any fairies you find.

You will need:
Double-sided tape, scissors and pretty wild materials.

1. Wind double-sided tape around your stick in a spiral, or stick it in rings around the stick.

2. Take your wand on an expedition to collect pretty fairy things, like fallen petals, soft leaves, fluffy seeds and white feathers. Stick them along the sticky tape.

3. Large petals can be cut into strips and shapes and stuck on the wand.

You will need:
Tiny twigs, fine wire, petals, seeds and flowers.

Magic fairy wands

1. Hunt for straight flower stems or tiny twigs with smooth bark.

2. Thread little petals, seeds and tiny flowers along some fine wire. Twist the wire round the wand, adding more decorations as you wish.

Each season, make a fresh wand with new wild treasures.

Star wands

Natural star wands are made from freshly cut green bendy sticks about 1 m (3 ft) long.

You will need:
A large green bendable stick (willow is perfect), thin wire.

1. Make a bend in the stick about 30 cm (1 ft) from the thicker end, and then make three more bends, each one about 5–10 cm (2–4 in) apart.

2. Straighten the stick, then fold it at the lower two bends to make a shape like a back-to-front number 4.

3. Thread the thin end of the stick back up through the triangle of the 4, pulling it through gently until you have made two points of a star.

4. Loop the stick round behind the sloping edge of the triangle and fold at the bend to make another point.

5. Wind the thinner end of the stick down the wand's handle and tie a knot or add some thin wire to fix it in place.

6. Decorate with fairy treasures.

Magical icicles

Discover the magic of a freezing cold day when the world is transformed into a glistening wonderland, perfect for ice elves and frost fairies.

Wrap up warm and get out icicle hunting. The best time to go is when a very hard frost follows a slight thaw. Every little drip will be transformed into a magical fairy wand or elf sword. Search for icicles beside streams, under roofs, hanging from twigs and anywhere that drips and drops of water may have frozen solid.

• Inspect icicles up close. Can you spot the magic energy trapped in the ice? Look for reflections and bubbles, or perhaps an electric-blue colour from reflected sky.

• Photograph as many fairy icicle wands or elf swords and daggers as you can, capturing their magic before they melt away.

• Collect a few icicles to take home and put in the deep freeze, ready to bring out when you need some chilly magic or a horn for a snowy unicorn (see page 145).

Hunt for fairy wings decorated with ice diamonds.

Elf armour and mini-weapons

Elf warriors are the fiercest, and most secretive, of all elves. They are careful to choose camouflaged armour so they can hide away from prying eyes.

Make your elf from clay and sticks, then gather wild materials for their armour and weapons.

This elf soldier is all ready for action, dressed in nutshell armour, with a spiky conker-case shield and a twig sword.

Can you make a miniature bow that can fire an arrow? Choose a bendy twig and attach a length of fine string or thread to make a curved bow.

This amazing elf warrior wears a suit of bark armour and is armed with a twig-and-string bow. Tiny arrows with feather flights are kept in a quiver made from a hollow stem. He also has a thorny staff.

Dressing up

To be accepted by real fairies and elves as a friend, you must use all your wild skills, think small and transform yourself into one of them. But remember, real elves and fairies don't like plastic and glitter – they prefer all things natural and recycled.

Wings for fairy friends

If you fancy flying off for fairy adventures, these wings are just what you need.

You will need:
Four bendy green sticks, each about 1 m (3 ft) long, string, wool, wire, elastic cord and wild fairy materials.

Willow wings

Natural wings blend perfectly into the wild fairy world.

1. Loop each stick to make a wing shape. Twist the thin end round the thicker end to secure in place.

2. Arrange the wings on the ground with two on each side and the ends all joined in the middle. Tie the ends together securely with thin wire or string.

Wire wings

If you can't find suitable bendy sticks, use a couple of old wire coat hangers (acceptable in the fairy world).

You will need:
Two wire coat hangers, a pair of old tights, gaffer tape and double-sided tape, elastic cord and some wild fairy materials.

1. Bend the coat hangers into circles, gently working the wire to remove kinks as best you can.

2. Bend the circles gently but firmly to make matching wing shapes as shown. Fold the hanger handles in on themselves; tape them together so no sharp edges are sticking out.

3. Cut the legs off the pair of tights. Stretch one leg over each wing, arranging the toe section over a wing tip. Tape them together, as shown.

They are best made in the spring with bendy newly growing green stems of willow and hazel.

3. Wind coloured wool around each wing to make a pattern.

4. Weave leaves, grasses or other wild materials through the wool to decorate.

5. Slip two loops of elastic around the centre of the wings, ready to put over your arms so you can fly away!

5. Add two loops of elastic, as with the willow wings.

4. Wind and tie the extra fabric over the join between the wings, covering all of the tape.

6. Decorate with flower petals and leaves stuck on with double-sided tape.

Seasonal crowns for fairy queens and Kings

Make twig and green leaf crowns in spring, petal or buttercup crowns in summer, golden leaf crowns in autumn and spiky crowns in winter.

Vine crown

This crown is woven from the long tendrils of a vine, decorated with a few garden flowers.

Goosegrass crown

Goosegrass, also called cleavers, is a common creeping plant. The little hooked hairs on its stems stick it to other plants and itself, perfect for bunching together to make fairy crowns. Weave a few flowers around it for an instant wild fairy crown.

Buttercup crown

Gather common wild flowers, such as buttercups, to weave a delicate fairy crown.

Becoming an elf

Elves are skilled at hiding in the wild world and making wild weapons. To join them, you'll need to practise your camouflage skills (see pages 26–27), weave a shield and a crown or hat, and carve a simple stick sword or dagger.

Leafy elfin headdress

A great way to help you blend into their world. Weave a crown from bendy willow and weave ivy and other wild materials through the willow.

Sword or dagger

Elves are champion protectors of the wild world. Go into the woods to choose a strong magical stick for a sword or a dagger (see swords page 62).

You will need:

Strong straight sticks, bendy sticks, raffia and leaves.

Woven shield

1. Carefully bend the sticks to make a shield-shaped frame, tying the loose ends with raffia.
2. Tie some straight sticks across the frame in both directions to make a stick mesh.
3. Weave long fresh or dried leaves in and out until you have filled in the whole shield.

Safety tip
• Take care when using knives – ask for a grown-up's help.
• Don't point sticks at people's faces.

101

Mini-worlds

Now you've found and clothed your fairies, it's time to enter – and help create – their mini-worlds. You may walk past trees in the park on your way to school or play by flower beds and bushes in the garden, but have you ever stopped to look more closely? Magical miniature worlds with forests of little plants and flocks of tiny creatures are waiting to be discovered everywhere outdoors.

So get the shrinking potion out of your magic cabinet and prepare for a wild mini-adventure. Go exploring with a magnifying glass – perhaps you will find a bumblebee helicopter, a molehill mountain or a fairy disguised as a beautiful butterfly. Look in grassy forests, damp mossy hills, mountainous anthills and tiny toadstools perfect for an elf to sit on.

Making wild mini-worlds

Can you find your way into a mini-world and make a welcoming home for fairies and elves?

Make a pebble pathway to show the way to a fairy doorway in a tree trunk.

Search for the perfect place. Look for hidden doorways, tiny windows, mossy rooftops and turrets or little pathways. Here are a few ideas for bringing wild mini-worlds to life:

An elf hideaway with a bracket fungus roof has a secret doorway and a ladder ready to pull up when everyone is safely inside. There is even a high window just right for spying on enemies.

Go out in cold wintry weather to make a snow fairy's cottage; this one has a walled garden with a wooden gate and trees made of dead flower heads. The door and windows are made from dried stems.

104

This ancient elf fortress is protected by a multi-headed beast. Can you spot the throne with its mossy cushion, some delicate wings hung up to dry and a table set for a feast?

Tempting treats

Tempt wild fairies and elves into your miniature world by leaving them special gifts.

They may like some wild edible berries on a leaf, new wings carefully tied up in a leaf parcel or a beautiful fairy outfit with a beech nut helmet.

No fairy will be able to resist the taste of wild strawberries.

New wings will always come in handy so are bound to be a draw to the fairies.

Safety tip
• Never eat wild berries unless you are absolutely sure they are safe for you and the fairies to eat.

No self respecting fairy would pass up the chance of a beautiful new outfit.

Fairy feast

**Fairies just love parties and feasts! Prepare a magical tea party
with a beautiful table ready to welcome the tiny guests.**

A low tree stump makes a perfect table, surrounded with cone stools. This table is set with
leaf plates, acorn cups and grass-stem knives. A leaf tablecloth is covered in walnut and
snail-shell bowls laden with a feast of delicious fruits, flowers, nuts and seeds.

Miniature beach worlds

Discover fairy and elf worlds at the seaside or on beaches beside lakes and rivers. Bring them to life with a little magic and wild materials collected from the shore line.

Hidden doorways

Can you spot pathways through the seaweed leading to hidden fairy or elf doorways? This doorway, protected by green seaweed curtains and a hooked crab's claw, hides a secret fairy cave.

Making beach fairy dens and gardens

Use wild beach materials to make magical dens and gardens for little people to discover…

Hidden among the pebbles of a river beach, this little elf cottage with a wooden doorway would make the perfect home for a secretive elf.

This tiny teepee of twigs and stems makes a perfect camping spot for a fairy.

Beach fairies may love to discover an enchanted garden full of wild treasures such as shells, old coral and seaweed.

Make a
beach outfit

Just like their woodland friends, beach fairies and elves love to dress up. This outfit includes a beautiful seaweed dress decorated with shells and other beach treasures, plus a fairy staff and a whistle (music is very special to fairies).

Make a holiday home

We all need a holiday now and then, when we can stay in an exciting new place and share new adventures. Fairies and elves enjoy relaxing in a holiday cottage with an enchanted garden, or going on a magical mystery tour to a secret destination.

1. Fill your container (such as a flower pot, a basket or a seed tray) with soil or compost.

2. Decorate with twigs, pebbles, leaves and other tiny wild materials.

This elf garden has a tent made from eucalyptus bark and is being visited by bird pets.

You will need: A container, wild materials, clay and some string.

Here are a few ideas for how to decorate your holiday home…

This wooden holiday cabin has bark walls, and a door with a doorknob and bell. The beautifully tended garden is full of flowers, and petal clothes hang from the washing line.

In this enchanted fairy garden, a pebble path leads to a wooden bench, a swing and a shell swimming pool with a diving board.

Outside the cabin there is a table set with an acorn bowl full of tasty treats.

Fairy flowers

Growing scented wild flowers and herbs rich in sweet nectar makes any garden a perfect holiday destination for fairies. The flowers will attract butterflies, bees and other nectar-feeding insects. Perhaps one of them will offer a lift to the fairies, who often hitch a ride when travelling long distances.

Can you spot the flower fairy walking along the path before she takes a refreshing dip in the pool?

Tiny explorers

Help explorer elves and fearless fairies discover new worlds for themselves in natural sailing boats and rafts. Launch them across a pool, a puddle, a stream, or a rockpool at the seaside.

Making little boats

Can you send your boats off on a journey and then bring them safely back to shore?

1. Make little boats from bundles of twigs, rushes or reeds, tied together with string.

2. To make the boats seaworthy, add a keel to stop them tipping and a sail to catch the wind. And remember to check that they float.

3. Tie each boat on to a long piece of string so you can drag them along in the water, bringing them back when you need to.

4. Make a safe place for a stick and clay elf or fairy captain to sit.

If you find this, please send me a message

If you can find a yellow waxy leaf, that would be perfect.

Leaf or bark messages

Everyone loves the idea of discovering a message in a bottle washed ashore by the tide. But leaving glass or plastic bottles in the wild world is not a good thing to do, as they can harm wild creatures. Here is a better way to send wild world secret messages.

You will need: **Leaves, bark, and a permanent marker.**

1. Use a permanent marker pen to write a message for the fairies or elves on a tough waxy leaf or some papery bark.

2. Make the leaf into a sail or a flag for your boat.

3. Set your message boat adrift on the water. Perhaps another explorer will discover your message and send you a message in a boat in reply!

Safety tip
• Always have a grown-up with you when exploring near water.

A marker pen like this will work well.

113

Monsters

Think of a monster and what do you see? A huge, scary, ugly creature? Or something small, friendly and even beautiful? Monsters come in all shapes and sizes. We all see them differently.
You will find your own monsters out in the wild world, brought to life by your own imagination.
Open your eyes and discover monsters hidden among trees, in the clouds, on the beach or at the park.

Tree monsters

Tree time is slow time, different to human time. Trees may live for hundreds and hundreds of years, growing gradually, reaching for the sunlight and stretching their roots deep into the soil. They offer shelter and food to many plants and animals while they stand and watch the world go by, waiting for us to turn our backs so they can reveal their hidden monsters.

Tree monster hunt

Hunt for monsters among trees in the deep dark woods or at the park. They are hard to spot, but their eyes can give them away.

In winter, look for spooky, dark silhouettes or see how a blanket of snow may reveal a monster. In summer find leafy monsters buzzing with life.

Is that hole a hungry mouth?

Is that branch a
muscly arm?

Is that knot in the
bark a beady eye?

Photograph monster trees and doodle
faces on top of the photos. Write a
story about your tree monster. What
does he look like? Is he old and gnarled
with wrinkled skin? What has he seen,
standing there for all of those years?

117

Bringing tree monsters to life

Find an interesting tree, and use nearby wild materials to create a face. Will it be friendly or will it be so terrifying it scares away other monsters?

Look for places to put stones, chalk or flints to make eyes and teeth, or add funny clay faces to knobbly bits of bark.

A rotting log can be transformed into a crocodile with stick legs and a leafy eye.

A low curving branch could become a snake-like monster. Bring it to life by sticking leaves on with clay and drawing details with chalk.

A fall of snow reveals more monsters, like this one, hidden in a fallen branch. With added leafy nostrils and long rush eyelashes, it comes alive.

Beach monsters

Take your imagination to the beach. What can you discover hiding in the sand, in rock pools or among pieces of sea-sculpted driftwood?

Monster clues

Hunt for evidence. Long ago, ancient monsters were transformed into fossils, and are now hidden among rocks and stones. Look carefully and you may discover a real fossil monster.

Can you find other monster clues? Patterns on rocks may be scaly skin or a stone might be a monster's head.

This rock monster looks friendly.

Shell and sand monsters

This sea serpent was moulded in sand and brought to life with a scaly skin of shells.

Driftwood monsters

Hunt for monsters in sea-worn branches thrown up on the beach by the waves. Bring them to life with pebbles, seaweed and other wild beach materials.

Pebble and stone beach monsters

A simple collection of shells and pebbles can be transformed into your very own monster, just like this friendly-looking creature basking on a rock.

Use patterned pebbles to give your monster eyes, a nose and a mouth.

This stone monster looks like it's swimming through the shingle of the beach.

Large stones can be turned into a dinosaur-like creature lying in wait on the beach.

Small pebbles can be decorated with mini-monsters – perhaps a tightly curled sea serpent.

Draw features – such as eyes, noses and mouths – on separate pebbles to create mix-and-match faces, like this scary one-eyed creature staring up from the ground.

Draw the details with a pencil or a piece of charcoal.

Shadow monsters

Do you ever see monsters lurking in the shadows? The most cunning monsters only reveal themselves to human eyes as mysterious dark shapes or spooky reflections. Create shadowy monsters on sunny days or after dark in the light of a torch, using a natural canvas of bark, sand, snow or water. Try photographing them without showing how they have been created.

Transform your shadow into a monster

On sunny days, your shadow is your constant companion, following you everywhere. It will evolve throughout the day with the movement of the sun. Use your body to make crazy monster shadows to photograph.

Add sticks or leaves to make ears, horns, antlers and other funny details.

Experiment with shadows of your whole body (or just your hands) on tree trunks, on the ground or on snow.

Monster reflections

Discover monsters reflected in the natural mirrors formed by puddles, pools and ponds on windless days. Make funny monster reflections using your arm or a stick decorated with wild materials.

Sandy shadow monsters

Sunlight on a sandy beach is perfect for shadow monsters, which change shape as the sun moves across the sky. Look carefully and you may spot them everywhere!

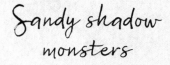

Discover shadow monsters at the park

Look at the shadows cast by a park bench like this one, or a slide or rubbish bin. Can you add objects to transform the shadows into monsters?

The more you look, the more shadow monsters you'll see.

← When held at the right angle, this normal-looking twig turns into a scary shadow monster.

Stick and leaf shadow monsters

A collection of sticks and leaves may look nothing like a monster; until you see its shadow. Make these funny little monsters on white paper against a wall or at the beach by casting shadows on the sand.

Cloud monsters

Test the limits of your wildest imagination by looking for fluffy monsters floating among the clouds or in reflected sky on a wet sandy beach.

Get looking

Lie on your back in a big open space on a sunny windy day when the sky is dotted with fluffy white clouds. Look up though half-closed eyes – what can you see? Photograph the clouds. The monsters may be easier to spot through the eye of a lens.

Let your imagination run free. Can you see a long-nosed witch riding on a broomstick, a cloud-eating dragon or maybe an ogre with a runny nose?

Splodge monsters

Wild-ink splodge monsters

1. Splatter wild ink on to paper to make some random splodges.
2. Mix a little bicarbonate of soda with lemon juice in a bowl. See how it fizzes and grows!
3. Pour drops of the lemon mixture over the wild-ink splodges, then watch as the colour slowly changes to blue.
4. How many monsters can you spot in the ink splodges?

Let them dry in the sun before drawing in a few details, such as teeth and eyes.

Mud splodge monsters

1. Scoop up some muddy water on the paintbrush and splatter it over the paper. Tip the paper so the muddy water moves around to make crazy shapes.
2. Let the splodges dry. Can you spot muddy monsters?
3. Draw on details with a thick black pen.

Can you see the battling splodge monsters?

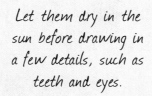

127

Monster feet

Make huge monster feet for you and your friends in winter snow or in sand at the beach. Be sure to leave a space at the back of each foot so you can step into them and become a monster. You never know who might come along and try them on for size!

Snowy feet

1. Push snow into big plastic boxes to make blocks.

You will need: Big plastic boxes, trowel or beach spade for carving details, and wild materials.

2. Turn the blocks out in your chosen monster spot, and then carve into feet.

3. Add twig claws and other leafy decorations if you wish.

Once you've got the feet made, why not use snow to create the rest of the monster too?

128

Sandy feet

1. Drag sand into big piles and sculpt them into huge feet. Are they for a giant bird or a yeti?
2. Add wild beach materials, such as mussel shell toenails or razor clam claws.

Remember, wet sand near the shoreline is easier to mould than dry sand.

Monster footprints

Most wild creatures are shy and difficult to spot. Sometimes, we only know they are there at all because of the clues they leave behind. Play a trick on your friends by leaving a trail of monster prints.

2. Or you can make your own track moulds indoors in a plastic box lined with clingfilm and a layer of clay. Use a stick or your finger to make a monster footprint in the clay.

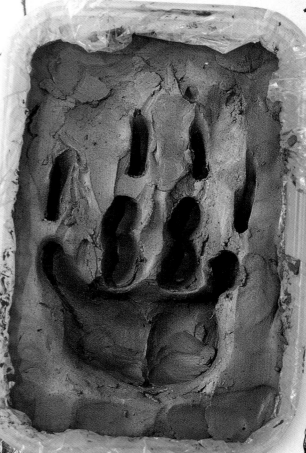

Muddy monster footprints

1. Go outside in search of squidgy mud. Look for animal tracks and use a stick to change them into monster tracks, perhaps by adding longer toes and bigger claws.

What fearsome creature made these tracks?

You will need:

A stick, plaster of Paris, plastic tubs, water, a spoon, some clay and clingfilm.

4. Pour the plaster of Paris mixture into the track, then add a thick layer of plaster on top of the track.

5. Leave to harden for at least 20 minutes. Carefully remove the set plaster cast from the mould and then gently peel off the mud or clay.

3. Pour plaster of Paris into a plastic bowl, add water and mix slowly to make a smooth yoghurt-like mixture.

Be sure to space your footprints out, so it looks like your monster has very long legs.

6. Let the plaster cast dry overnight. Take it outside and make a monster print trail. The top one could be a dragon, while the one on the left looks more like a jabberwock.

Monster footprints in the snow

You will need:
Waxed cardboard, waterproof pens, string, gaffer tape, scissors, hot glue and a pair of wellies.

1. Put a welly on the card, then draw the outline of a footprint with three long claws around it.

3. Cut out the toes.

These footprints were made from waxed cardboard, but have fun experimenting with other materials from the recycling box, such as flattened-out juice cartons.

2. Roll up some card to make the outer toes and add strength.

Remember to add a claw at the back of the foot.

Use your pens to colour in the nails at the end of the monster's claws.

Be sure to press your monster feet right down into the snow to make good, deep footprints.

4. Cover the front of the middle toe with another piece of card so you can push your welly into it.

5. Tie the monster feet onto your wellies with string. But if your wellies are old, sticking gaffer tape over the string will fix the monster feet in place more securely.

6. Now walk through the snow to leave a trail of monster tracks behind you!

Transform yourself into a monster!

Experiment with natural body paints, transforming yourself into a scary monster!

You will need:
Natural chalk, clay, charcoal, berry paint (see page 45), pestle and mortar, water and paintbrushes.

1. Collect natural chalk, or soil with a high clay content. You can also experiment with charcoal and berry paint.

2. Grind the chalk or charcoal in a pestle and mortar and mix with water to make a gloopy paint. Mix clean clay-rich soil with water to make a brown.

3. Use paintbrushes and sponges to paint your arms, legs and face (taking care to avoid your eyes and mouth). What kind of monster will you become?

Paint a skull on your face, and bones on your hands and body to turn yourself into a human skeleton.

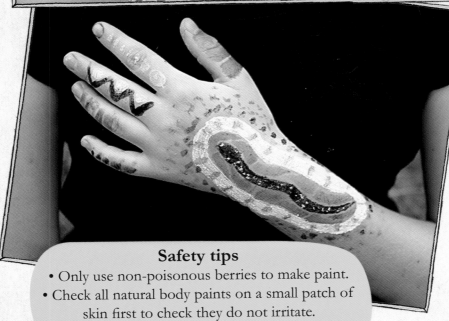

If you don't want to paint your whole body, you could paint a monster on your hand.

Safety tips
• Only use non-poisonous berries to make paint.
• Check all natural body paints on a small patch of skin first to check they do not irritate.
• Avoid painting near eyes and mouth.

Mythical beasts, mermaids and giants

The amazing beasts
and creatures from
myths, legends and
fairy tales are generally
very friendly – so long
as you keep on the right
side of them!
The mermaids,
unicorns, giants and
other mythical Wild
Things in this chapter
are a cunning blend
of reality and your
own imagination.

Mermaids

Mystical mermaids and mermen are both fish and human, meaning they can live under the sea and on land. At the seaside, look out for nature's magical mer-people, such as dolphins, seals, sea lions, otters and whales. If you enjoy being both in and out of the water, make yourself a sandy tail, and sit in the waves as a mermaid until the waves wash your tail away.

Hunt for evidence of mermaids

The beautiful long-haired mermaids of myth and legend love treasure and jewellery. Look out for the mermaid clues they leave behind, and make your own mermaid treasure chest…

Sponge to apply make-up

Driftwood wand

Perfume pots

Mermaid's false nails and nail holder

Seaweed hairbrush and comb

Scales lost from a mermaid's tail

Jewels made from wave-washed glass

Mermaid's purses

138

Table for a mermaid feast

Mermaid's never wander far from the sea, but this feast on the rocks might tempt them out of the water. A starter of shellfish on a stone plate with a bread roll will be followed by a main course of seaweed pasta, fish and caviar, served on a shell plate. The feast can be washed down with a salty drink in a shell goblet with a straw.

Board games

After the meal, mermaids may like to play noughts and crosses or board games on the rocks, using shell and pebble counters. Can you make up your own beach board games?

Mermaid's dressing table

Find a special place hidden among the rocks for a mermaid's collection of jewels and make-up. Display sea-washed glass jewels in shells, and look out for a make-up sponge, perfume bottles, hairbrush and comb. You can also put sand make-up in shells.

At the beach, transform wild beach treasures into mermaid jewellery and hair decorations, or take a few treasures home to make some longer-lasting mermaid mementoes.

Draw patterns on shells with marker pens.

Decorate hair clips or rings with pretty shells and dried seaweed, sticking them on with hot glue.

Make a bracelet or a
necklace by threading
string or leather cord
through shells with holes in.

For mermaid make-up, mix sand with a
few drops of food colouring to create blusher,
eyeshadow or cleanser.

Safety tips
• Take care at the water's edge.
• Hot-glue guns should only be used
under close supervision.
• Sand make-up is for mermaids only —
don't use on human faces.

Unicorns

Unicorns are among the most beautiful and magical of the woodland creatures, but they are also the hardest to spot – and almost impossible to catch! Their single horn fizzes with powerful spellbinding magic.

4. Find a shorter stick for the unicorn's horn. To make a truly magical unicorn, find a wild horn with superpowers. This might be a stick covered with ancient moss or lichen, or with thick protective supernatural bark or perhaps an unusual twisted shape.

3. Push the long stick into the open end of the sock up to the heel.

You will need:

Old socks, newspaper, string, double-sided tape, hot-glue gun, and wild materials, including a long stick.

Make a hobby unicorn

Use nature's magical wild materials to make your own unicorn to protect you from all those bad monsters out there. Ride your unicorn through an enchanted forest or in a secret wild place at the park. You never know where its magic will take you!

1. Start by choosing a sturdy stick for your hobby unicorn. It should be just the right size for you to ride on – and strong enough to withstand some pretty rough play.

2. Now choose an old sock for the unicorn's head. Stuff scrunched-up newspaper into the sock to make a head shape.

Stick wild materials on with double-sided tape or hot glue to make eyes, nostrils, a mouth and ears. Perhaps your unicorn would also like feathery decorations or a leafy mane.

5. Cut a hole in the sock's heel near the top of the long stick. Push the long stick a little way through the hole and tape the horn onto it, as shown. Now push the long stick back into the hole so you can only see the horn.

6. Tie the open end of the sock around the long stick to secure it in place.

Use a forked stick to make a two-headed unicorn — with double the magical power!

Safety tip
• Hot-glue guns should only be used under close supervision.

Magical unicorn horns

These tasty ice lollies double up as multi-coloured unicorn horns! Keep them in the freezer ready for a snowy day.

You will need:
Plastic freezer bags with handles, tape, cardboard, chopstick, food colouring, elderflower cordial and berry juices (see pages 42–43).

1. Turn a plastic bag into the shape of a unicorn's horn. First, fold the bag in half and press along the fold. Open the bag up again.
2. Fold one side of the bag at an angle towards the central fold line. Then do the same with the other side.
3. Tape the sides of the bag in place, and then fold each side in again and tape in place. You should now have a long thin triangle shape.

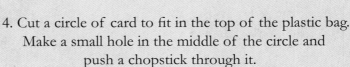

4. Cut a circle of card to fit in the top of the plastic bag. Make a small hole in the middle of the circle and push a chopstick through it.
5. Place the card and chopstick in the bag.
6. Add some coloured elderflower cordial or berry juice to a depth of about 5 cm (2 in), and hang the bag from a tree or washing line on a cold night – or in the deep freeze – until frozen. Then add another layer of colour. Keep adding more layers of different colours (and different flavours), and leaving to freeze until you have a long multicoloured ice horn.
7. When you are ready to use (or eat!) your unicorn horn, dip it in warm water and then peel the plastic bag off the ice. In summer, it makes a tasty magical ice lolly, while in winter you can use it to decorate a snow unicorn or cast a colourful spell.

Hold your horn by the handle.

Snow unicorns

On a snowy day, create a pure white unicorn, carving out front legs, a body, and a head with a mane and long ears. As a final magical touch, add the multicoloured unicorn horn you made earlier.

Giants

The grizzly giants of fairy tales shake the earth with their footsteps, shout with voices like thunder and enjoy munching small children for breakfast. Thankfully, these sorts of creature are very rare. But we encounter giants every day. It's all a matter of where you are in the scale of things. From the point of view of a tiny ant or a bee, you are a huge scary giant with massive clumsy feet and eyes that never see enough. Next time you take a walk in the wild, remember to tread lightly and watch where you put your feet.

Giant heads

This amazing giant's head can be found at the Lost Gardens of Heligan in Cornwall, England. Create your own giant heads using fallen trees, sand at the beach or snow.

Tree root giant

This giant emerges from the roots of a fallen tree, brought to life with leafy eyes, sticks for teeth, and branches and grasses for hair.

Snowy giant

After a heavy snowfall, look for the top of a giant's head; the starting point for this giant was a pile of rocks on a hillside. Bring your giant to life with twiggy hair, stone eyes, a sticky nose and snowy teeth.

Shadow giants

When the sun is very low in the sky, shadows lengthen to become long-legged giants. Make yourself into a huge giant in the golden sunlight of autumn or on snow in winter. Take photos of different giant shadows in different places.

Can you spot this shadow giant's scary beast hound?

Sleeping giants in the landscape

In enormous wild landscapes, it is easy to imagine giants lying silently among rocks, hills or mountains.

Can you find giant clues? Is a long pond really a giant's footprint that has filled with water, or is a single huge rock a giant's marble?

Is this just a split rock, or a pair of massive giant hands saying a prayer, with rainbow power beaming out from between the fingers? Can you find natural wonders so enormous in scale that it's easy to imagine they may have been made by a giant, or are even part of a giant?

Magic protection

Are you brave enough to turn to the next chapter, which is all about scary, dark creatures? Get prepared by practising some protective magic inspired by mythical beasts.

Magic eyes

Worried that a Wild Thing might look at you with its evil eye to deliver a curse? Make these magic eyes and place them for protection on a favourite den or tree. Try a clay eye decorated with leaves, sticks and a shell pupil, or make a snow eye with moss and twig details.

Wild gargoyles

Have you ever spotted carved human and animal faces on the roofs of buildings? These are gargoyles, fantastical creatures which protect buildings from harmful spirits (and they also carry water coming off the roof away from the walls below). Make your own clay gargoyles (the uglier the better!) to protect your house, your den or even a favourite tree.

Masks

A wild mask may help to scare away Wild Things and evil spirits. The coloured leaves of autumn make perfect mask decorations.

1. Take the plain mask, cover with foil and make the features bigger using clay or plasticine.

2. Cut cardboard to make ears, horns or a spiky headdress, and stick these to the top of the mask. Cover the whole thing with foil.

You will need:
A plain plastic or cardboard mask, clay or plasticine, silver foil, cardboard, PVA glue, leaves and other wild materials.

Bright red leaves make a dramatic mask.

3. Cover the mask with wild materials, such as colourful leaf pieces, sticking them on with PVA glue.

Dreamcatcher

Scared of bad dreams, or the dark creatures that cause them? Hang a wild dreamcatcher in your window, outside a den or in a tent doorway to trap them. Traditional dreamcatchers were made of small willow hoops woven with a web-like mesh of horsehair or string, decorated with feathers and beads.

You will need:

A bendy twig, wool or raffia, and wild materials.

1. Cut a green twig of willow or hazel, bend it round into a circle and tie in place with raffia or wool.
2. Weave raffia or wool around the hoop to make a spider's web pattern.
3. Decorate with feathers, teasels, lichen, twigs, leaves, shells or whatever wild treasures you can find.

A bleached skull to ward off any bad spirits

Prickles to snag on a monster's fur

A gnarled witch's finger to curse away unwanted bad thoughts

A magic unicorn's horn to produce a safety force field around your bed

Monster snowball mobiles

Transform snowballs into Wild Things to hang on a mobile, in a tree or outside a window. What funny creatures can you create?

> ### You will need:
> **Several very short twigs about 5 cm (2 in) long, string, wild materials – and some snow!**

1. Tie a length of string around each twig, and then wrap snow around each twig so you have several snowballs on strings.
2. Decorate the snowballs with wild materials to make faces or amazing creatures.
3. Tie the Wild Thing snowballs along a stick and hang up until the snow melts and the Wild Things disappear.

Feathers make great ears.

Wild Thing totem pole

Create your own wild totem pole with the Wild Things that are most special to you. Perhaps your totem pole could protect your den, go in a plant pot on the patio or be left in a favourite wild place.

> ### You will need:
> **A good strong stick with knobbly bark, clay and wild materials.**

1. Push the stick into the ground while you decorate it.
2. Wrap lumps of clay around the stick in three or four places. Mould each lump into a face.
3. Add wild materials to bring the faces to life.

153

While you are snuggled up in your cosy bed at night, the wild world comes alive outside in the darkness. Persuade your grown-ups to let you stay up late and go out for some exciting adventures. Be brave, go to places away from electric lights and use your skills to discover the dark Wild Things as they emerge from their hiding places. It can be a little scary – but there is so much to discover.

Like most wild animals, trolls (big, ugly and a bit stupid) and goblins (small and mischievous) prefer to be left alone. If you ran into a troll, it would be just as afraid of you as you are of it. Go out after dark with some goblin and troll protection, but keep your wits about you (and take a grown-up). Are you ready for the challenge?

Goblins, trolls and the dark creatures

Nature's dark creatures

The Wild Things of the night use magical powers to survive. Their big ears hear the tiniest sounds, their sensitive noses sniff out the slightest scent, while their eyes make the best use of any available light. Go out as darkness falls. When the birds are singing their goodnights, find a good spot and sit there, quiet and still. Listen, smell and let your eyes adjust to the gathering darkness. Remember, many minibeasts are more active in the dark when the birds that eat them are asleep, so look for snails, slugs and woodlice.

Looking in the dark

Always take a torch but try not to use it – wild creatures are disturbed by our bright lights. Let your eyes adjust to the darkness until you find your natural night sight. Very quickly you will be surprised by how much you can see. If the darkness is complete, use a head torch with a red beam (see Wild Skills page 16). You may spot animal eyes watching you right back.

Recording sounds after dark

At dusk, find a place to sit quietly and tune in to nature's sounds. Listen for rustles in the undergrowth, birds calling, mammals barking, frogs and toads croaking. As it gets darker the sounds will change. Record them on your mobile device.

Shine a coloured torch at trees in the woods and at the park. Does the light reveal hidden trolls and goblins?

Night-time track trap

Wild Things don't realise they leave telltale footprints behind. Discover which dark creatures (or trolls and goblins) are prowling around after dark in the garden, the park or at the woods ith this track trap.

1. Check the weather forecast. This activity won't work when it's pouring with rain!

2. Fill the tray with sand, add water until the sand is wet enough to form a smooth layer when you gently wiggle the tray from side to side. The sand must be firm enough to hold an imprint, so drain off any excess water and sprinkle on a little more dry sand if need be. You could use a thick layer of clay on a tray or wooden board instead.

3. Put a little cat food or dog food on the sand or clay.

4. Go outside just before dark and find a little pathway that might be used by wild creatures. Place the track trap on the pathway.

5. Go back next morning – have you trapped any tracks? Perhaps a hedgehog, a deer or even a goblin? Photograph the tracks and see if you can identify them.

6. Try the track trap in different places. How many different tracks can you trap?

The track trap on a woodland pathway

A clay track trap

This track trap caught a goblin unawares. It trapped his tracks but he also left behind some green nasal hair, the remains of a snail snack, a hairy wart, some flaky green skin and scattered cat food (goblins are such messy eaters!).

Spooky lights of the night

Some plants and animals possess the magic power of "bioluminescence" which lets them make their own spooky light. On a night-time safari, you may be lucky enough to spot…

• The neon-like gleam of glow worms
• Fireflies sparkling like fairies among the trees
• Toadstools softly glowing among rotting leaves
• At the seaside, the waves may glow with "phosphorescence" – light from microscopic plankton. If you encounter this rare event, try a night paddle in the glowing water to see your legs lit up in the inky black sea.

Phosphorescent plankton have turned the sea a shimmering blue.

Safety tips
• Check tides and only swim in safe places with grown-ups present.
• Never touch toadstools, as they can be highly poisonous.

Night birds

Owls have magical powers that help them hunt at night. Using their huge eyes and very sensitive hearing, they pinpoint the rustling of mice and voles in the undergrowth. They fly silently, so they can swoop down and surprise their prey. You are unlikely to see owls because of their amazing invisibility powers, but listen for their loud calls.

Magical moths

Summer days are the time for beautiful butterflies, but summer nights will reveal magical moths with delicate wing patterns and feathery antennae. Parks and gardens can support hundreds of different moths, attracted by flowers that release their scent after dark. To discover more about magical moths, set a tree trap. They just can't resist this beer and sugar potion.

1. Heat the beer in a saucepan.

2. Remove from the heat and stir in the sugar until is has dissolved.

3. Add the black treacle, mix together and then leave to cool.

4. Put the mixture in a container with a lid.

5. Go outside just before dusk. Paint the mixture onto tree trunks or fence posts at eye level.

6. At dark, go out with a torch and look at the sugar traps. How many different moths can you spot enjoying the sugary treat?

Bats

Are bats nature's darkest creatures? These mysterious winged mammals of legends and spooky tales have amazing magic powers, using echolocation to hunt down tiny insects in total darkness (see page 21). The best time to see bats is just as dusk is falling. You may spot them leaving their daytime roosts to swoop to and fro in search of insects over gardens, parks, rivers and woods. Or look out for them in towns, chasing moths attracted by street lights.

Goblin and troll hunting

How do you know a goblin from a troll? It can be tricky, but in general:

- Goblins – hang around in gangs, go on raids and live in lairs underground, rather like badgers. They love treasure and shiny things, so don't leave anything lying around!
- Trolls – bigger than goblins and only come out at night (they turn to stone in daylight). They prefer caves and underground places, hollow trees and the spaces under bridges.

Trolls and goblins are the messiest of Wild Things, with warty itchy skin, always sneezing and coughing and leaving lots of nasty clues behind…

Be prepared

Masking your human scent will confuse goblins and trolls. Don't wear freshly washed clothes. Instead, carry a smelly concoction (see page 164) and a mini-goblin or troll to protect you from the real ones.

Goblin and troll lairs

To uncover goblin or troll hidey holes, look out for ancient hollow trees, exposed roots that create hiding places, a dark spooky cave, a damp mossy hollow or underground holes.

Goblin and troll scavenger hunt

Once you've found where they live, go on a hunt to look for disgusting evidence that they might be hanging around. Look for…

A back scratcher and bits of flaky skin.

Scabs – small bits of red and brown which they have picked off.

Green nasal hair and slimy snot – from a troll or goblin sneeze.

Dried spit – look for yellow or pale green splodges on bits of bark.

Poo – don't touch but the stink will tell you if its troll or goblin poo.

Warts (green or hairy), which often drop off when they rub against tree trunks.

Used toothpicks – they often get rancid food stuck between their teeth.

Toenails – their nails grow so fast they always need clipping.

Also look out for treasure – may include shiny rubbish, as they aren't always very good at telling real treasure from rubbish! And favourite snacks, such as juicy slugs and snails.

161

Find a troll bridge

Look for little bridges across streams or ditches. Can you creep across without disturbing the troll? Or leave a scary troll or goblin puppet (see opposite page) on a bridge to distract them so you can cross safely!

This scary goblin puppet should scare any troll, allowing you to cross safely.

Sweet treats to keep goblins and trolls away

Goblins and trolls absolutely hate sweet things. Leaving a sweet treat like these wild raspberries will stop them coming out of their dark smelly lair!

Make your own wild goblins and trolls

You will need: Spiky sticks, clay and wild materials.

1. Collect scary wild materials: look for empty snail shells, spiky thorns, bleached bones and bird skulls, and fluffy seeds.

2. Wrap a large lump of clay around a spiky stick and mould it into an ugly face.

3. Add wild materials: thorns, sharp sticks or stones make good teeth, or fluffy seeds can be a little beard.

4. To make your puppet really convincing, add warts, scabs, slimy snot and ear and nose hair. Or how about giving it one eye? Or three eyes? Or several ears? The uglier the better!

5. When you come across a real troll or goblin, get your puppet to do all the talking to distract them until sunrise!

Scary puppets

A troll or goblin puppet may frighten real trolls and goblins away if you meet them in the deep dark woods. How scary can you make yours?

Snow troll and goblin challenge

The challenge is to make snow goblins and trolls in the most unlikely places to take your friends by surprise or to protect your home from winter's dark Wild Things.

Try making a car troll: find a snow covered car (preferably one that belongs to your grown-ups), carve out eyes, add a big nose and a big scary mouth.

163

Goblin and troll nastiness

Goblins and trolls get up to all sorts of nastiness, but perhaps you can beat them at their own game!

Smelly concoction

Dark creatures have sensitive noses. Make a smelly concoction and carry it with you to mask your human smell and protect you as you hunt for them. This may confuse them into thinking you are a troll or a goblin.

1. Each person makes their own concotion in a jar.

2. Choose some gloopy and smelly wild materials and mix them together in your jar.

3. Share your concotions. Close your eyes and take a good sniff of each one – which is the smelliest and ugliest?

Troll or goblin soup

Time to make a tasty mixture from the nasty goblin and troll clues you collected on your scavenger hunt – such as green nose hair, scabs, flakes of skin, and toenails.

Have fun mixing the wild materials with mud and puddle water. No goblin or troll will be able to resist it!

Safety tips
• Always wash your hands with soap after playing with mud and other wild materials.
• Don't collect dead animals or poo.

164

Make troll snot

It may sound disgusting, but this is
an amazing mixture to play with!

You will need:
**Cornflour, green
and yellow food
colouring, a plastic
bowl, a spoon
and water.**

1. Take everything outside, as this
is a very messy activity.

2. Put some cornflour in a bowl
and add water. Mix it well to
make a gloopy mixture.

3. Add food colouring
to make a suitably
snotty colour.

4. Have fun experimenting
with the mixture. If you
get the consistency just
right it will go hard when
you squeeze it but drip
slowly between
your fingers as
you release
the pressure.

This troll is producing
quite a lot of snot
of his own!

Night adventures and moon magic

Just because the sun has gone down, that doesn't mean it has to be totally dark. There are plenty of ways to bring a little wild light into the darkness.

Full-moon adventures

Head to a wild space on a full-moon night to discover some moon magic.

As the full moon rises, look for silvery reflections and magical pathways leading across the water – in puddles, streams, lakes or the sea. Ask an adult to help you collect some shimmering reflection water in a little bottle, ideal for a magic spell.

Make spooky moon shadows of yourself or your troll and goblin puppets (see page 163).

If it's a cloudy night or there isn't a moon, use a torch to make spooky shadows.

Magic lanterns

Light up night-time adventures with a spooky monster, goblin or troll lantern. It's perfect for a festive parade or a Halloween celebration.

You will need:
Bendy lengths of willow, coloured tissue paper, masking tape, PVA glue, black pens, and glowsticks or small torches.

1. Make the lanterns indoors. Build the basic shape from willow, taping it together with masking tape. Make a sturdy base so you can attach a torch or a glowstick.

The giant glowing mouth of this monster lantern makes a spooky light, enough to frighten away any real monsters!

2. If you wish to carry your lantern, attach a willow loop or some string firmly to the top.

3. Cover the willow frame with a layer of tissue paper, sticking the sheets together with slightly diluted PVA glue. Let the paper dry and then add one or two more layers to strengthen it.

4. When the glue has dried, use more tissue paper and a black pen to add staring eyes, a red nose, big teeth and other goblin and troll features.

5. Light up your lantern and head out for an adventure.

Firelight magic

Keep the Wild Things at bay with a fire, while enjoying the warm glow and flickering light with friends and family. Some of the most magical outdoor experiences are those shared around fires, surrounded by darkness. But remember, only make fires when and where you have permission to do so and with grown-ups to help. The safest fires are those made in a fire pan or a pit. For further information on making fire, see the detailed Fire Safety tips on page 13. If you can make a safe fire, here are a few wild firelight ideas…

Discover dancing fire shadow spirits – dance in the light of the fire and film your flickering shadows.

Share spooky stories around the warming glow to keep the trolls at bay.

Watch the magical movement of the flames. Can you spot monsters and other Wild Things hidden among the glowing embers?

Safety tips
• Fire safety – see page 13 for details of making fires and keeping safe.
• Keep with other people when out at night.

Exploring the underworld

When we walk over the ground, its solid surface seems immovable. Yet beneath our feet an incredible underground world pulses with life. Plant roots push through the soil, fungi spread their long tendrils and little creatures squirm about feeding on decaying plants – and each other.

Make a wormery

Earthworms are nature's soil improvers, adding air and water by mixing up the layers and breaking down leaves and grass into humus which will help new plants to grow.

Soil recipe

Soil is nature's gold. It has the magic power to support all Wild Things. Without soil there would be no plants or animals. But what is soil? Can you make up your own recipe?

You will need:

Minerals (sand and clay), water, tiny plant materials, leaf litter, a bucket and a large jar or pot.

Be sure to handle the worms carefully.

1. Soil is made up of ground-up rocks (such as fine gravel, sand or clay) and humus (decomposing plants). Experiment by mixing together different amounts of the materials in an old bucket.

2. To test your soil, put some in a pot and sow some seeds. Will they grow?

1. Go on an earthworm hunt. They are more likely to come to the surface just after a shower of rain. Handle the worms carefully.

2. Put layers of sand, soil and dead leaves in a large jar. Add a few earthworms and sprinkle some leaves on the top.

3. Cover the jar but make sure air can get in.

4. Wrap black paper around the jar and leave it in a cool spot. Take a peek at the wormery each day to see if the magic is working. Are the layers getting mixed together?

5. After a week or two, release the worms back where you found them.

This shiny red strawberry has become a fuzzy grey lump.

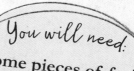

You will need:
Some pieces of fruit (such as strawberries or lemons) and jam jars.

Rotting recipe

If plants didn't rot down to make humus, there would be no soil and the world would be covered in a thick layer of smelly dead plants. But the magic power of decomposers, such as insects, fungi and bacteria, breaks plants down, returning their goodness to the soil.

1. Put a piece of fruit in each jar. Place the jars on a sunny windowsill.

2. Take photos to record the changes over about a week. You will see a difference every day as moulds grow and spread, breaking down the fruit.

3. Use a magnifying glass to investigate the moulds. Some will be green and flat while others will be white and fluffy or spiky.

4. Note how long the fruit takes to decompose into a sludgy mess.

5. Compare various fruits and vegetables. Do different moulds grow on them?

Safety tips
• Keep the rotting fruit in the jars until you dispose of them in a compost bin.
• Wash your hands after touching the worms and fruit.

Disappearing logs

Go to the woods or the park and hunt for fallen trees and branches. Rotting wood provides food and homes for some of nature's unsung heroes. Turn a log over and see what you can find. You may spot beetles, centipedes, millipedes, woodlice, snails, slugs and other creepy-crawlies – they're all part of the magical process of improving the soil so that more Wild Things can grow.

Remember that each log is a wildlife home. Always put them carefully back as you found them.

Living leaf litter

Have you ever walked through magical carpets of autumn leaves, enjoying the swish as you kick them in the air? The layer of leaf litter over the woodland floor provides food and shelter for all sorts of little plants and animals.

Using a trowel, collect some leaf litter in a plastic tray. Gently look through the leafy material to see what little Wild Things you can spot. Take a closer look with a magnifying glass.

Safety tips
• Take care when looking under logs and exploring leaf litter.
• Always wash hands thoroughly after handling these materials.
• Wear gloves if there is any danger of poisonous mini-beasts or plants.

You will need:

A very large jar, soil, rotting wood, leaves, kitchen roll, an elastic band, and some snails and slugs (best to look for them on a wet day).

Make your own mini-underworlds

Discover more about some of the underworld's little Wild Things by making mini-underworlds so you can watch them more closely.

Snail settlement

Follow the daily life of snails and slugs.

1. Put some moist soil, rotting wood and leaves in the jar. Add some snail food, such as lettuce leaves or vegetable peelings.

2. Find some slugs and snails and put them in the jar. Then attach two pieces of kitchen roll over the top of the jar with an elastic band so the slugs and snails can breathe – but can't escape!

3. Keep your snail settlement in a cool place, and make sure the soil stays moist. Spy on the slugs and snails to see how they eat. Perhaps they will lay eggs.

4. After a couple of weeks or so, return the slugs and snails to where you found them.

You will need: **A plastic container, soil, bark, leaf litter and stones.**

Woodlouse world

These little Wild Things love dark places and rotting wood.

1. Put a layer of soil in the tray. Use a seed tray or plastic box – the sides need to be slippery so the woodlice can't escape.

2. Add some bark, leaf litter and stones.

3. Collect a few woodlice – look for them under logs and stones.

4. Put the woodlice in the plastic container and let them settle in.

5. Keep an eye on the woodlice world and see where they choose to go and make their home. Spray the soil with water occasionally so it doesn't dry out.

6. Return the woodlice to where you found them after a few days.

Index

Thanks and acknowledgments

We owe a big thank you to everyone who helped us to make Wild Things a reality:

- Our agent Alice Williams who believed in this project from the start.
- The team at Lonely Planet, especially Andy Mansfield whose wild imagination and design skills made this book truly magical.
- Pete Williamson, whose illustrations brought the Wild Things to life.
- All the young people who explored wild places with us and introduced us to their Wild Things.
- The University of Oxford Harcourt Arboretum and the Lost Gardens of Heligan in Cornwall where some magical photographs were taken.
- Our husbands Ben and Peter and our children Jake, Dan, Connie, Hannah and Edward who have grown up to become intrepid wild explorers.
- The fairies at the bottom of the garden and the friendly troll in the hollow tree up the road, without whose friendly advice this book couldn't have been created…

Additional photo credits: p12 Shutterstock/javierDan, p39 Shutterstock/TunedIn by Westend61, p45 Shutterstock/grey_and, p58 Shutterstock/Al Redpath, p59 Shutterstock/Eric Isselee, Shutterstock/ Zety Akhzar, p146 The Giant's Head, Lost Gardens of Heligan © 1998 Pete Hill & Sue Hill, peteandsuehill.co.uk, p156 Shutterstock/EcoPrint, p158 Shutterstock/WUT.ANUNAI, Getty/ watcherFF, Shutterstock/Ryan M. Bolton, Getty/DEA/C. GALASSO, p159 Getty/De Agostini Picture Library